With a Humble Heart

Dennis Binns

ISBN 978-1-64492-282-8 (paperback)
ISBN 978-1-64492-283-5 (digital)

Copyright © 2019 by Dennis Binns

All rights reserved. No part of this publication may be reproduced, distributed, or transmitted in any form or by any means, including photocopying, recording, or other electronic or mechanical methods without the prior written permission of the publisher. For permission requests, solicit the publisher via the address below.

Christian Faith Publishing, Inc.
832 Park Avenue
Meadville, PA 16335
www.christianfaithpublishing.com

Printed in the United States of America

Introduction

HAVE YOU EVER WONDERED how we should pray? Would it not be best to receive our answer from the Lord himself? In Matthew 6:9–13, he tells us, but most people believe that all we need to do is recite the Lord's Prayer.

> This, then, is how you should pray: "Our Father in heaven, hallowed be your name, your kingdom come, your will be done, on earth as it is in heaven. Give us today our daily bread. And forgive us our debts, as we also have forgiven our debtors. And lead us not into temptation, but deliver us from the evil one. For Yours is the kingdom, the power, and the glory forever and ever. Amen."

Have you ever really dissected the prayer itself? The beginning of the prayer is of thankfulness and glorification. Next comes the intercession or requests. The ending is once again that of thankfulness and glorification.

The prayers in this book are written with that in mind as well as acknowledging the Trinity. For those that may be unfamiliar, when I begin each prayer, there are titles I give for the Trinity. For example, Great Spirit refers to the Holy Spirit, Almighty Healer refers to Yeshua, and Creator of all things refers to God the Father.

A Pondering Moment

Awakening

We have gone through the twentieth century that filled us with lies, deception, and half-truths. We should now spend the twenty-first in facts, love, and understanding. We all have our faults. We all have our own addictions or thorns as I call them. We need to reach that level of being able to look past what we see and begin to use our other senses. All are not of the light. Many live in the darkness. If we look upon the character, the actions, and the words, we will get better understanding.

Learn to love. Learn to listen to the spirit. No longer should we allow anyone to control what you eat, wear, believe, etc. We are all unique individuals, created by the Creator of all things. We all have been given a purpose and a path unique to each individual. Always be aware that one is never alone. Speak through the spirit when you are confused, down, needing guidance, or just feel like sending up praise.

Movements have started to protect the very necessities of life, from being destroyed by corporate and government greed. Idle No More began a few years ago in the northern part of Turtle Island. Now the shell part of the island indigenous people stand to protect the land and waters from the same. They are the native peoples from diverse tribes that began standing together with the nation at Standing Rock, North Dakota. Though the players may be different, the result is the same. How long must we stand up to protect our waters, air, and land? We need to turn the tide and clean up what we have nearly destroyed. We need to also bring pressure to our leaders to start working on alternative sources of energy instead of bringing more destruction to the environment. After all, if we continue on this path, there will be nothing left to save ourselves.

Stand up now for all you believe without fear. Be the light. In peace, we can achieve anything. In violence, all will be lost. Make no mistake, we are now at that fork in the road where we must choose life or death. That one direction that continues on through technology and how we have lived our lives to present. The other in a complete reset, knowing and understanding our original duty to the Creator. If you still do not understand, research the Hopi Prophecy that is now staring us in the face. We all know that we can no longer live this way. At least, this is what I have hoped we have learned. Be blessed, my friends.

A Pondering Moment

Being Too Busy

While we spend time trying to place more things in our day, running to and fro, performing business, or ensuring that no time is wasted, we never leave time to observe or learn from all things that come to us. We spend too much time providing for the family or buying things to make us happy. But we find ourselves saying there is never enough time in the day. We chase after materialistic dreams only to find more misery and—ultimately—our own destruction. We have become selfish into thinking that the world owes us something instead of us owing the world.

We all have a purpose, and it isn't about our desires. We are connected together to give assistance to all living things. From the two-leggeds, four-leggeds, swimmers, fliers, and crawlers, to the plants, trees, and waters, we are connected. We must learn to be compassionate and bring healing to all things. We must become the caretakers we were meant to be.

Take time out, away from our concrete jungles and experience nature. It is nature that we need to observe. For through our observation, we may find new knowledge and wisdom. Nature nurtures and heals if given the opportunity. Many plants and herbs found in nature have healing properties to all our ailments, diseases, etc. All we need to do is observe and learn.

We need time of reflection and tranquility. We miss too much in life when we keep ourselves occupied within the routine of our working lives. We wake in the morning, work during the day, come home, sleep. Day after day is generally the same. Why not take time and truly relax and enjoy life?

Be blessed, my friends.

A Pondering Moment

Changing The World

THERE IS NO HONOR in violence. It only brings more of the same, and nothing gets done. Its only production is hatred, discrimination, and heartbreak. If we want to change the world, we must use peaceful means. For it is through peace that changes occur and spreads throughout so long as the heart is willing.

Take for instance, Standing Rock. The violence you see from the law enforcement side is not reciprocated from the protector side. The cause is just and has become a movement worldwide. It is not about the land and water just in North Dakota. Water is the lifeblood of all living things. Greed does not care. It only serves its master.

Though the battle was won temporarily, the war still rages on. All over the world, governments are allowing the black snake (oil pipelines) to inhabit sacred lands and areas where the people do not want it. If we are to protect the waters from future disasters, then we all must take a peaceful stand and say, "Enough!"

Not everyone is able to stand on the frontlines. But that doesn't mean one cannot be active in getting the word out, sending supplies, praying, donating to legal funds, etc. We are all in this together, and we are all united to bring about change.

Be blessed, my friends.

A Pondering Moment

Charity

WE MUST HUMBLE OURSELVES because we are no better than the next. We all have our trials to endure; even the wealthy tend to live in misery. To heal the soul and feel peace is to help those around us. If you see someone on the side of the road requesting help, please offer it if it is something you can do. Even a kind word works wonders. Cook for the needy if you are able. Offer your services without thinking of a reward. This is what a spiritual being ought to be doing rather than working toward our own selfish desires, isn't it?

I look upon those with signs asking for money, and it grieves me not to be able to give that day. It should not matter if these people are truly needy or not, in my opinion. For those that aren't will eventually fall, but those that are will be blessed with another day of life and happiness. We do entertain angels unaware here on earth. Who's to say that we don't drive or walk by them every day? Follow your heart, follow your spirit, help those in need, and always offer up prayers of thankfulness.

Paying kindness forward. Have you ever noticed the feeling you receive inside when you have helped someone in need? That should speak to you that you have done the right thing. To walk away without assisting others does not bring such a euphoric feeling. Compassion should not be something that is done once in a while. It should be something for us to do as often as possible. Do you agree?

Be blessed, my friends.

A Pondering Moment

Choices

OUR LIVES HAVE BEEN geared around the choices we have made. From the time we are born until the time of our passing, choices have been made by us on a daily basis. No one is born with a preconceived notion of how our character is going to be or what direction life will take us. It is through the choices we make.

No one is born a certain way. We may have strong feelings toward something, but we choose to act one way or the other. Whatever we come across each day requires a choice. We can either choose the right path or the wrong one. If we make the wrong choice, we should not blame anyone else on the choice we made.

One can also choose to believe in something or not. We can choose to believe in the law of opposites or not. One can choose to believe in evolution, for example, and disregard creationism or even believe in a heaven but not Hades. It is a choice we stand by individually.

Our character is built upon the choices we make. So it would behoove us to take time to think about our choices before we act upon them.

Be blessed, my friends.

A Pondering Moment

Choose One or the Other

Some say that their God is not a vengeful God. He would never anger or cause hardship. Obviously they have not studied his Word, in my opinion. Does not a father discipline his children when they have done wrong? Has not some gone so far as to disown, for a time, his children that continually disobeyed and turned their backs to him? And does he still not love them unconditionally? But through his discipline, hope they will find the error of their ways, and ask for forgiveness?

When he created us, it was in his image. Not only his image, but I believe we also were instilled with his emotions. Yes, Yahweh is also an emotional God. How else could he love us? When we stray from our path and his laws, would he not get angry and discipline us? When he loves unconditionally, would he not welcome his children back into the fold?

In my mind, we have two choices in life. Either follow God or follow Satan. There is no in between. If you are not following his Word and being one with his Word, you are following Satan whether you choose to believe it or not. Some will say they are atheists and follow no God. Then they have been deceived by the evil one.

Some say that the Allah they follow is the true God. Study the history. Allah is a moon deity. So they too have been deceived. Does it mean that I hate Muslims? No, of course not. I love all people. I love all that Yahweh created. To not love them is to not follow his

Word. Hate the sin that the flesh gives us but love the person. But Allah and Yahweh are not the same God as the evil one wants us to believe—one of Satan's great deceptions.

John 14:6 tells us "Jesus answered, 'I am the way and the truth and the life. No one comes to the Father except through me." So if you want to get to the Father, you must believe in his Son, repent of your sins, and ask him to come into your heart.

Be blessed, my friends.

A Pondering Moment

Connection to God

There are times in our lives when we feel alone, lost, or confused. Times when we are misunderstood or are surrounded by darkness. One must learn to believe that there is a higher power, a Creator, a God that is aware of all things. Learn to understand that the spirit that dwells within us, connects us with the Creator and all living things. We are truly never alone. There are those connected to us that can help, and there is always an answer given by the Spirit if we only trust in him.

Please, never think that you are alone. Many have gone through some of the trials that you experience. Seek insight or answers to your questions. Don't allow emotions to control you. Be confident in knowing that you are never alone and that you have a special unique purpose in life. You have a path that needs to be followed. Search your spirit and communicate with the Creator. The more you do this, the more connected you become.

Be blessed, my friends.

A Pondering Moment

Fighting Principalities and Powers

"For we wrestle not against flesh and blood, but against principalities, against powers, against the rulers of the darkness of this world, against spiritual wickedness in high places" (Ephesians 6:12)

When we fight or wrestle with principalities, we are not fighting against rulers of this world. We are fighting against superhuman agencies, angelic or demonic spirits that manipulate those rulers—those spirits that man cannot see with the naked eye. Yes, those powers or entities that exist even when you cannot see them.

The best way to combat them in our fleshly bodies is through prayer and the faith that goes with it. We have diverse orders of the angels of God that assist in fighting off the evil one's forces. Our prayers, in my opinion, aid them in their quest.

So remember, when you read reports, listen to news, think of what powers may be influencing the rulers of our day, whatever manipulation the demonic or dark angelic entities work on us can be combated through God's intercession. For Yeshua to intercede, we need to pray with conviction, belief, and thankfulness.

Why do bad things happen to good people? I suspect for two reasons: One, God wants us to get to a place where we can learn and grow from the lessons he sends us. And secondly, the evil one uses his dark entities to manipulate us and attempt to draw us away from God.

Be blessed, my friends.

A Pondering Moment

Ignite the Fire

A TRUE CHRISTIAN KNOWS that where there is a heaven, there is also a hell. Many preachers will refrain from speaking of Hades (hell) in hopes that they will keep their pews filled. A church that does not preach the good and the bad and is not spirit-filled is a dead church. If you are in a church that is not spirit-filled, find one that is. We must stop being lukewarm and start being hot for the Lord.

Now I know there are some that don't want to hear about hell. But it does exist. How many near-death experience testimonies are out there that have shown this? Too many to count. Just because we cannot see what is before us doesn't mean it doesn't exist. But because many cannot believe in something or someone standing before them, they choose to ignore.

A true Christian knows we are in the last days. This generation will see the prophecies of the Bible unfold as some have already. This generation will see the oldest city, Damascus, fall overnight into a ruinous heap. This generation will see the oncoming war, proclaimed in the Bible, between the evil coalition that is forming now that will go against Israel. And this generation will find Israel still standing when the dust settles. Man cannot destroy what God has blessed.

Rise up, brothers and sisters, and allow the fire from within to burn again. Time is short, and there is much work to be done. Don't be lukewarm in your belief and your works. There are many that need you. Remember the Beatitudes and follow them. Be compassionate to all. Hate the sin but love the sinner as Yeshua did during his time on earth and now in heaven. Study the word and begin to truly understand the message. Both Old and New Testaments work in conjunction with each other.

Be blessed, my friends.

A Pondering Moment

Kids and Pets

LET THEM BE WHO they are!

Let kids be kids. Let your pets be pets. Why do we continue to be either overprotective in the child's case or dress up our pets like kids? Why don't we allow our kids to play outside like parents did in the past? Why do we insist that they stay inside the home or in the backyard? Let them get dirty, muddy, and grass-stained. The earth has healing properties, and it doesn't take much to clean them or their clothes. I would know since I have spent years as the Mr. Belvedeer of the household. Children need to grow up learning how to live in the environment. Yes, they'll be protected in the house and smart around computers. But how much will they lose not growing up discovering nature?

And why do we dress our pets up? This makes little sense to me unless they have either a skin or fur problem. Why do we insist on parading them around in dog shows? Pets are great companions, friends, and even sometimes, our children. Nothing wrong with that, but they are our pets. Let them be what they are. Bathe, feed, pet, and comfort them. They do a lot for us, let us do the same for them. Allow them to be what they are—our friends! Not pets at a costume party.

Be blessed, my friends.

A Pondering Moment

Leaders

WE SPEND OUR TIME criticizing those leaders we elect without realizing that perfection does not inhabit these bodies we were born with. Perfection can only be found within the third heaven. We are given the responsibility, however, to elect those that will bring us forward along our paths. Although we are unique in nature, we have all strived to become better than we are. We need to choose our leaders to govern and lead us in a more righteous direction.

In life, we have our peaks and valleys. We are sinners and, occasionally, fail to follow the path we are given. There are times when we stray and focus upon worldly matters rather than upon the divine. We are to look toward God daily. We have failed in keeping a commitment of constant communication with God through prayer. And it is then that we fail to elect those in office that should be leading us toward a better life.

When we stray and lose our focus, we elect those that do not have our best interest at heart. We receive those that cause division or reverse the direction of our path. It is God that chooses our leaders. Some are anointed, some are not. Those that are anointed are known by their works toward peace and a more prosperous lifestyle. Those that are not bring instability through deception and lies. We need to get ourselves to a time where we pray often and keep our focus upon godly things.

Be blessed, my friends.

It is He who changes the times and the epochs; He removes kings and establishes kings; He gives wisdom to wise men and knowledge to men of understanding.

—Daniel 2:21

A Pondering Moment

Lies and Deceptions

WE HAVE GONE THROUGH the twentieth century that filled us with lies, deception, and half-truths. We should now spend the twenty-first in facts, love, and understanding. We all have our faults. We all have our own addictions or thorns as I call them. We need to reach that level of being able to look past what we see and begin to use our other senses. All are not of the light. Many live in the darkness. If we look upon the character, the actions, and the words, we will get better understanding.

Learn to love. Learn to listen to the spirit. No longer should we allow anyone to control what you eat, wear, believe, etc. We are all unique individuals, created by the Creator of all things. We all have been given a purpose and a path unique to each individual. Always be aware that one is never alone. Speak through the spirit when you are confused, down, needing guidance, or just feel like sending up praise.

Movements have started to protect the very necessities of life, from being destroyed by corporate and government greed. Idle No More began a few years ago in the northern part of Turtle Island. Now the shell part of the island indigenous people stand to protect the land and waters from the same. They are the native peoples from diverse tribes that began standing together with the nation at Standing Rock, North Dakota. Though the players may be different, the result is the same. How long must we stand up to protect our waters, air, and land? We need to turn the tide and clean up what we have nearly destroyed. We need to also bring pressure to our leaders to start working on alternative sources of energy instead of bringing more destruction to the environment. After all, if we continue on this path, there will be nothing left to save ourselves.

Stand up now for all you believe without fear. Be the light. In peace, we can achieve anything. In violence, all will be lost. Make no mistake, we are now at that fork in the road where we must choose life or death. That one direction that continues on through technology and how we have lived our lives to present. The other in a complete reset, knowing and understanding our original duty to the Creator. If you still do not understand, research the Hopi Prophecy That is now staring us in the face. We all know that we can no longer live this way. At least, this is what I have hoped we have learned.

Be blessed, my friends.

A Pondering Moment

Perception

LIFE IS NOT ALWAYS about how we perceive it; same as death. One can believe that what they see around them is nothing more than spiritless everyday living with no beauty that can be seen in their eyes. Or they may see darkness and evil around every turn. Some will believe that there is no Creator, that what surrounds them is nothing more than things without a spirit.

There are those that live life believing that they are the very center of the universe, and all things revolve around them. They spend their days seeking entitlements and respect because they believe they have earned it simply because of the lives they've lived. There are those that look no deeper than the color of one's skin to judge them without knowing the trials they have endured. Then there are those that are proud and boastful of their accomplishments in life, not knowing that their view of success has been skewed by those that came before them. Some presently judge an entire group merely by the horrendous transgressions of those in the past.

How can we judge another without knowing their background or the character within them? How can we walk through the urban streets among the homeless and not feel compassion? How can we truly believe that just because of our trials, skin color, or misfortunes that we are owed or entitled to that which is not ours? How can we not be in awe when we are in nature and discover life outside of the concrete jungles?

How can we go through life thinking that creation is either a myth or magic when all around us, we are able to see the works of the Most High? Do you not know that there is beauty even in the storm?

Be blessed, my friends.

A Pondering Moment

Unique Paths

We all have our own unique path, given to us by the Creator. There are times when we may not understand what another is doing, or what they are thinking, or even why they believe the way they do. There is no reason for anyone to fully comprehend another since the paths are not the same. Unless we have walked in another's shoes, felt what they have felt, seen what they have seen, or endured the same trials, true understanding can never be fully comprehended. It is because of our uniqueness that our paths run differently. But they all are guided by the Creator if we allow it.

Everything has a purpose. Everyone has their own belief system. Try as we might, we may never fully understand. But we must take the time to try to see from another's point of view. Without this, we will continue the cycle of unforgiveness and the hardening of hearts. We must never lose sight of who is always in control. Nothing happens without a purpose or a reason.

It is good to have friends that will understand or at least be open enough to respect the other. Of that, I am truly grateful. We may not see eye to eye on certain topics, but we can always respectfully agree to disagree. It does little good to harp on certain things when there are far more important things to strive for. One person cannot obtain peace without having the assistance from others. One person can form an idea for positive change, but it takes a following in order for that change to occur.

Be thankful for our challenges, for without them, we cannot continue to grow. Be blessed, my friends.

GREAT SPIRIT, ALMIGHTY HEALER, and Creator of all things, with humbled hearts, we gather together to offer up many thanks. We thank you for the gift of life given to us. May we use it for the purpose you have mandated. We thank you for our paths and the Sacred Spirit that will guide us through life. We thank you for our elders that teach us lessons for the present as well as the wisdom of the ancestors. We thank you for our children that will carry the wisdom and lessons to the next generation. We thank you for our friends that remain with us throughout our trials.

We ask for guidance during times of confusion and misunderstanding. We ask for strength when we are low in spirit. We ask for your healing hands to be placed upon those that continue to suffer through diverse diseases and disorders. We ask for a greater spirit of unity among your children during this time so we may begin the arduous task of bringing back balance. We ask for an end to the things that continue to divide us. May we learn to love and respect each other. We ask for an end to war in a world where we are deeply weary of the violence and disrespect shown throughout the four corners. We ask for an end to government and materialistic control and ask for greater freedom to do that which must be done. We ask for hardened hearts to soften, closed eyes to open, and veils of secrecy to continue to be lifted. We ask for an end to the hatred, greed, lust of power and money. We ask for freedom for those who have been incarcerated for a crime they did not commit. We ask for greater understanding of all that surround us. We ask for guidance, peace, and strength be given to those that have lost hope and are reaching out to others. May they be given your words of encouragement and sympathy to get them through the rough times. We ask for greater compassion for those that are homeless or are struggling in the reservations located throughout this country.

We thank you for the wisdom found in the winds. We thank you for the mountaintops that give us the rushing pure waters to hydrate us. We thank you for our daily food and ask for its blessing. We thank you for the rain forests that provide us with the air to breathe. We thank you for all two-leggeds, four-leggeds, swimmers, fliers, and crawlers that surround us. May we endeavor to give them the respect they deserve. *Emenv.*

GREAT SPIRIT, ALMIGHTY HEALER, and Creator of all things, it is with a humbled heart that we gather together to offer up many thanks. We thank you for the warm winds of summer that brings warmth as it clears out the stagnant air and resupplies with the good. We thank you for the soft cold blankets of snow in the winter. We thank you for the soaring of eagles as they soar above the storms. We thank you for the rains that have provided water to thirsty lands. We thank you for those that plant the seeds in the spring to bring about a harvest by the autumn months. We thank you for the snowcapped mountains that bring us the rushing waters to hydrate our bodies. We thank you for the wondrous mysteries of the universe that surround us. For the tranquility we feel in nature, we thank you.

We ask for an end to the turmoil that surrounds us. We ask for protection, courage, strength, and compassion in these last days. We ask for your healing hands be placed upon those that are suffering through disease, disorders, and ailments. We ask for a bountiful harvest this year to provide food for the hungry. For the low in spirit, we ask for comfort and guidance. We ask for forgiveness when we have strayed from our path. We ask for patience when we begin to feel too anxious and start to act before we think. We ask for an end to the hatred and misunderstandings that divide your people. We ask for protection, strength, and guidance as we stand against those that would further destroy more of your creation. We ask for a time of peace, tranquility, and greater understanding toward all things. We ask for an end to the abuse and violence against our women and children. We ask for hardened hearts to soften, blind eyes to see, and closed minds to open so we may begin to bring unity among the four colors across the four corners. We ask for greater compassion toward the poor and the homeless. Where there are closed doors of opportunity, we ask for their opening. We ask for a change in mindsets so all may begin to see the destruction we have caused and the courage to change. We ask for strength and motivation for our leader as he continues to shed light upon the corruption found in our government.

We thank you for our many trials that strengthen our spirit. We thank you for the support we receive from family and friends during our journey. We thank you for the elders that teach us the importance of the environment and of humility. We thank you for our children that continue to remind us of innocence and lessons long forgotten. We thank you for the music found in the winds and waters that soothe our restlessness. We thank you for the gift of life and the many blessings you have given us. *Emenv.*

GREAT SPIRIT, ALMIGHTY HEALER, and Creator of all things, it is with a humbled heart that we come together to offer up many thanks. We thank you for the beauty of the salmon as it defies the odds and swims upstream to spawn. We thank you for the waters cascading down from the mountainside that give us the necessary hydration for our bodies and that of all living things. We thank you for the knowledge that we are created from the earth and, therefore, a part of her. We thank you for the worms and ants that aerate the soil, allowing for new growth. We thank you for the stillness of the lakes and oceans in the early morning hours as the sun slowly begins to spread its golden hue.

We ask for greater compassion toward the homeless, poor, widows, and children within the confines of our country first, lest we forget them. We ask for your miraculous healing hands to be placed upon those suffering through the many diseases, disorders, and ailments. We ask for truth to replace the deception perpetrated by those in power. We ask for a time where we can unite together without the hatred, misunderstanding, and greed that divides us from our brothers and sisters. We ask for protection for the defenseless, from the animals that inhabit the lands, mammals of the seas, to the people that are suffering through domestic violence and abuse. We ask for an end to our addictions that separate us from our true path. We ask for a cleansing of our spirits and strength of true knowledge, to replace the negativity we have allowed to remain for too long. For those that are low in spirit, we ask for strength, comfort, and courage be granted to them.

We thank you for the warm summer days as the children play and families come together to celebrate life. We thank you for the shades of the elm, maple, oak, and weeping willow trees. We thank you for the nutritious fruit on the branch, bush, and the vine. We thank you for the four seasons that show us that life also goes through its changes. We thank you for those that may come into our lives for a short time to bring insight and to show us those things that we may have forgotten. We thank you for the precious gift of life and the experience you have granted us. We thank you for the knowledge that even in our darkest hours, you are there when we call upon you. *Emenv.*

GREAT SPIRIT, ALMIGHTY HEALER, and Creator of all things, it is with humbled hearts that we gather together to offer up many thanks. We thank you for the serenity of nature. We thank you for the rushing of waters that flow from the mountaintops to hydrate us. May we work to keep them free from pollution. We thank you for the wisdom that can be found in the trees when we learn to empty our minds and listen. We thank you for the gentle winds that flow over the grassy meadows. We thank you for the air supplied by the trees that allow us to breathe. May we endeavor to keep the rain forests intact long after the era of pollution is ended. We thank you for the stillness of the lakes and ponds in the early morning hours as they bring peace to our spirits. We thank you for the smell of the salt air as we gaze upon the graceful movements of the ocean waves. We thank you for the sounds of the gull as we watch the sunrise from the shore.

We ask for contentment to what we have without the pressure of needing more than what is needed to survive. We ask for an end to the greed that can be found throughout the four corners. We ask for protection, strength, and guidance as we stand against those that would continue to destroy all that you have created. We ask for clogged ears to open and closed eyes to see so that we do not lose our culture and heritage. We ask for greater unity where division among your people no longer exists. We ask for a greater spiritual awakening in a time of great turmoil. We ask for hardened hearts to soften and compassion to build so we may see and assist those that are in great need. We ask for a bountiful harvest of crops so we may be able to place food on the plates of all people. We ask for an end to the abductions of our children and women. We ask for an end to the violence against them as well. We ask for guidance each day as we continue along our paths. May we journey with strong legs and compassionate hearts. We ask for your healing hands to be placed upon those that are suffering through diverse diseases and disorders. We ask for patience when we feel frustrated. We ask for the cleansing of our hearts so we may better understand the messages more clearly. We ask for your direction to enter the minds of our leaders and sound judgements be made. We ask for courage and your words to be used at times when they are clearly needed.

We thank you for our elders that give us the wisdom and instruction to build a better future for our children. We thank you for the innocence and lessons long forgotten when our children speak. We thank you for the rains that come to bring moisture to dry lands. We thank you for the ever expanse of the universe that surround us and is the center of our being. We thank you for all answered prayers. We thank you for the guidance you have provided to those that look toward you and open their hearts to you. We thank you for the wisdom that can be found within. *Emenv.*

Great Spirit, Almighty Healer, and Creator of all things seen and unseen, it is with a humbled heart that we gather together to offer up many thanks. We thank you for the many signs and wonders shown above. We thank you for the knowledge that you are still in control of the present and future. We thank you for the peace and tranquility we find in nature, away from the turmoil and destruction around us. We thank you for those that you have brought forward to continue teaching that which has been hidden for too long.

We thank you for the many answered prayers of healing of the past, present, and future. We thank you for those that come to us in our lives for a short time to provide the insight we need. For the many trials we have endured, we thank you for the strength you provide and the knowledge that they are to prepare us for that which lies ahead. We thank you for our family and friends that give us the support we need. We thank you for all two-leggeds, four-leggeds, swimmers, fliers, and crawlers that interact with us each day. For the sky that keeps us safe from harmful radiation of space, we thank you. We thank you for the earth that provides us with hydration, nourishment, and cures to our aging bodies. We thank you for the plants and animals that give us the clothing necessary to survive. We thank you for our daily food and ask for its blessing. We thank you for the knowledge that all things have a purpose. We also thank you for the knowledge that those things that have been in secret will now begin to be revealed.

We thank you for your forgiveness when we have disappointed you. We thank you for your love even when we may have turned away from you. We thank you for your blessings when you have found favor with us and your discipline when you have not. We thank you for the many gifts given. May we use them as we should to glorify you. We thank you for giving us the strength when we are weak, courage when we are afraid, and comfort when we are in pain. *Emenv.*

GREAT SPIRIT, ALMIGHTY HEALER, and Creator of all things, it is with humbled hearts that we come together to offer up many thanks. We thank you for the beauty of the butterfly as it emerges from the cocoon. We thank you for the hummingbird as it hovers around the flower while collecting the nectar. We thank you for the fruits from the trees that nourish us. We thank you for the many herbs that you provide to give us the cures we need for our aging bodies. For the majestic mountains that overlook the forests and valleys below, we thank you. We thank you for the many species of life, from the bear to the clam, that you have placed upon the earth. We thank you for the sacred spirit you have given to all living things that will help guide and teach us in our daily lives.

We ask for miraculous healing to be granted to those suffering through diverse diseases, disorders, and ailments. We ask for forgiveness when we stray from our paths and transgress against your laws. We ask for a time where we spend more time in spirit rather than focusing our attention solely upon worldly things. There is so much violence and destruction that surround us, and we ask for a time of peace and tranquility where we can begin to understand those things that concern us. We ask for an end to the chains that bind and control us, preventing us from doing that which is just and righteous. We ask for an end to our addictions that keep us from fulfilling our tasks. We ask for love to enter in the hearts where there is only hatred. We ask for clarity as we take this time to search for truth. We are tired of the deceit that has kept us bound for generations, and we ask that all things that were hidden to continue to be brought forth for all to see. We ask for mercy when we have done wrong and clear guidance on our paths. We ask for guidance for our leaders so their decisions will be just.

We thank you for our children that remind us of the innocence we have lost. We thank you for our elders that remain to give us the lessons of the present and the wisdom from the past. We thank you for our daily food and ask for its blessing. We thank you for the many gifts you have granted us. May we use them in the manner they were intended. We thank you for our family that have assisted in making us the people we are today. We thank you for those that come to us for a short time to provide us with the insight we need. We thank you for your love, guidance, discipline, and forgiveness. *Emenv.*

GREAT SPIRIT, ALMIGHTY HEALER, and Creator of all things seen and unseen, it is with humbled hearts that we gather together to offer up many thanks. We thank you for all two-leggeds, four-leggeds, swimmers, fliers, and crawlers. We thank you for the rocks, clay, sand, soil and the uniqueness of each. We thank you for the sacredness of all life. We thank you for the forests, jungles, plains, deserts, and ice caps. We thank you for the waters that flow from the snow-capped peaks cascading down around the rocks and waterfalls to the rivers and lakes below. We thank you for the gentle breezes that caress our skin and bring a calmness to our spirit. We thank you for the air we breathe, food we eat, and waters that hydrate all living things.

We ask for guidance to be granted to our leaders during this turbulent time. May they choose carefully during the decision-making processes. We ask for your healing hands to be placed upon those that are suffering through diverse diseases and disorders. For those that have lost loved ones, we ask for your comfort to be granted to them during the grieving process. We ask for mercy toward those that have no regard for the sacredness of life. May they learn that all life is given as a gift and each is sacred. We ask for an end to the abduction and murders of our women and children. We ask for mercy for those that continue to follow you even in our darkest hours. We ask for a greater awakening for those whose hearts remain dormant. We ask for guidance each day for all that continue with love and compassion in their hearts. We ask for an era of peace and tranquility where true equality among your children are shown throughout the four corners. We ask for a time of rest so our earth can regenerate nature to where it was in the beginning. We ask for honor and integrity to once again enter in the hearts of our leaders. We ask for patience when we tend to rush into things. We ask for an end to the mining, drilling, fracking, smog, littering, and hazardous material leakage that has caused so much damage to our environment.

We thank you for family and friends that have given us the support we need along our journey. We thank you for our elders that give us the stories, wisdom, and instruction needed each day. We thank you for our children that have reminded us of the lessons we have long forgotten. We thank you for our trials that serve to strengthen and prepare us for that which lies ahead. We thank you for our thorns that prevent us from becoming boastful. *Emenv.*

Great Spirit, Almighty Healer, and Creator of all things, it is with humbled hearts that we gather together to offer up many thanks. We thank you for life that blossoms in the spring, for the harvesting of the grains in the summer, the beauty of the trees in the autumn, and the freshness of the snow in the winter. We thank you for the rains that have come to lands of thirst. We thank you for the lightning that provides the soil with the necessary nitrates. We thank you for all two-leggeds, four-leggeds, swimmers, fliers, and crawlers throughout the lands. We thank you for the freshness of the mountain spring waters. We thank you for the beauty of the butterflies as they flitter about. For the dancing fireflies during the evening hours, we thank you. We thank you for our daily food and ask for its blessing.

We ask for forgiveness. We have failed from the main task you have given. We have destroyed the lands, cut down trees without replacing them, polluted the air and waters, left debris to orbit around our Earth Mother, killed the animals for sport, and sought after our own fame and fortune. We ask for forgiveness of our debts, trespasses, and self-righteousness. We ask for a time where our hearts are filled with greater compassion for those less fortunate than ourselves. We ask for hardened hearts to break loose of the chains that bind them. We ask for eyes blinded by lust of power and greed, be opened to see the destruction we have caused. We ask for an end to the hatred and greed that have caused our children to fight in wars across the great waters. We ask for an era of peace where all four colors can unite and return to the original task you have laid before our ancestors. We ask for an end to the violence and abuse toward our women and children. We ask for the release of all political prisoners throughout the four corners currently imprisoned under false claims. We ask for an end to the corruption of our governments. We are weary, Father, of the lies and deceit of those in high places and ask for a time where they govern for the people and not for themselves. We ask for a strong foundation of this generation so we may give strength, wisdom, and knowledge to our children to build on. For those people that are oppressed by their government, we ask for strength, comfort, protection, courage, and guidance toward a more righteous system of governance.

We thank you for our elders that have given us the necessary wisdom and lessons to strengthen us. We thank you for our children that will take these and teach them to the next generation. We thank you for our trials that serve to strengthen our spirit and prepare us for the spirit world. We thank you for your love, compassion, strength, and forgiveness that we need as we travel along our path. We thank you for the many blessings and gifts you have given to your children. We thank you for the gift of life and the hope of a better world. *Emenv.*

GREAT SPIRIT, ALMIGHTY HEALER, and Creator of all things, with humbled hearts we gather together to offer up many thanks. We thank you for the gift of life and the blessings you have given to your children. We thank you for the majestic mountains to the calmness of the oceans during the early morning hours. We thank you for the music found in the winds and rushing waters. May we take the time to listen. We thank you for the mists floating down in the morning hours that bring nourishment to the thirsty plant life and the waters that hydrate all two-leggeds, four-leggeds, swimmers, fliers, and crawlers. We thank you for the colors of the autumn leaves to the beauty of the spring flowers. We thank you for the knowledge that life is found throughout all your creation. We thank you for all life that inhabit all throughout the land as well as in the oceans.

We ask for greater patience where we are slow to anger. We ask for greater humility when we tend to be boastful. We ask for greater tolerance when we tend to become angry or disagreeable to others. We ask for unity when we are divided. We ask for healing for both physical and spiritual infirmaries. We ask for your guidance and strength to be given when we are low in spirit. We ask for a time of peace in a world filled with violence and division. We ask for strength of will when we travel along our paths and that our eyes remain straight. We ask for an end to the violence and abuse being suffered by our women and children. We ask for a time where men become men and not boys that refuse to mature. We ask for responsibility to enter their hearts. We ask for an end to homelessness. We ask for greater compassion where we do not focus on ourselves as much as we should our brothers and sisters in need. We ask for the return of our children and women that have been abducted. We ask for an end to war and the return of our sons and daughters. We ask for strength, courage, and humility in these days of persecution and turmoil. May we have the courage to further bring the good news to the lost.

We thank you for your Word and all that you have created. We thank you for the knowledge that life does not end here. We thank you for the knowledge that all things have a purpose though at times, we may not understand. We thank you for the rain forests that provides us with the air to breathe. We thank you for our elders that give us the lessons we need for the present and the wisdom of the ancestors. We thank you for our children that remind us of lessons and innocence long forgotten. We thank you for your love, guidance, discipline, and forgiveness. *Emenv.*

GREAT SPIRIT, ALMIGHTY HEALER, and Creator of all things, it is with humbled hearts that we gather together as one to offer up many thanks for all that you have provided. We thank you for the songs of the wrens in the early morning hours. We thank you for the diverse colors of the wildflowers along the plains. We thank you for the early morning breeze as it gently caresses our cheeks. We thank you for the beauty of the butterfly as it emerges from its cocoon. We thank you for the strength of the sycamore and redwood as they stretch out to the heavens. We thank you for the beauty of the oak, maple, and birch during the autumn months.

We ask for rains to come to those areas of drought and where there may be fires that endanger lives. We have done much to bring displeasure to you over the centuries. We have brought destruction to the lands through our mining, fracking, and drilling, littered our lands, polluted our air and waterways. We ask for your forgiveness. May we return to a time when we were better caretakers of all you have created. We have not properly cared for the animals as we should. We have hunted for sport and trophies rather than for necessity. Again we ask for your forgiveness. We ask for your guidance as we return our focus back to you rather than continue the destructive ways of the world. We ask for transparency in the halls of our government and end the corruption throughout the four corners. We ask for the release of all political prisoners incarcerated over crimes they did not commit. We ask for the strengthening of knowledge toward our cultures.

We thank you for our elders that continue to bring insight and wisdom to the younger generation. We thank you for the children that remind us of the innocence we have forgotten. We thank you for rain forests that provide us with air we breathe. We thank you for the calmness of the waters in the early morning hours. We thank you for the four seasons that remind us of the cycle of life. We thank you for the knowledge that all of creation revolves in cycles. We thank you for your love, discipline, forgiveness, and blessings. May we bring honor and humility back into a world that has fixated itself on selfishness and arrogance. We thank you for all answered prayers. *Emenv.*

GREAT SPIRIT, ALMIGHTY HEALER, and Creator of all things large and small, seen and unseen, it is with a humbled heart that we unite together to offer up many thanks. We thank you for the small birds in the nest. We thank you for the diverseness of the fish in the seas. We thank you for the crab as it scampers about the rocks on the shore. We thank you for the calmness of the waters in the early morning hours. For the trees that give us the oxygen from the carbon dioxide that allows us to breathe, we thank you. We thank you for the clouds that bring the rains to areas of need. We thank you for the lightning that supplies the nitrates to the soil.

We have transgressed much against you and ask for your forgiveness. We ask for calmness and tranquility in a world of chaos and destruction. We ask that the veil be pulled further apart so we may see more that has been hidden. We ask for patience when we tend to do things ourselves rather than awaiting your time of accomplishment. We ask for mercy, Father, for those times we have forgotten to focus upon you instead of the world around us. We ask for love where there is hatred, peace where there is conflict, understanding where there is confusion, and transparency where there is deception. We ask for miracles for those that are despondent and searching for relief. We ask for healing for those that are suffering through diverse diseases, disorders, and ailments. We ask for a time of peace where all we find is terror, war, and violence. We ask for protection of the defenseless. For those without hope, we ask for patience, charity, loving counseling, and your grace be upon them.

We thank you for the ocean waves that gracefully stretch upon the sandy shore. We thank you for the cool gentle breeze as it softly caresses our skin. We thank you for the beauty of the whale and dolphin as they break the surface of the ocean waters. We thank you for all four-leggeds, two-leggeds, swimmers, fliers, and crawlers that inhabit the earth. We thank you for your forgiveness, love, patience, and blessings that you have provided us. *Emenv.*

GREAT SPIRIT, ALMIGHTY HEALER, and Creator of all things, it is with a humbled heart that we gather together to offer up many thanks. We thank you for the knowledge that having dominion over the land and animals does not mean that we can do anything we want with them. We thank you for these times where the veils of deceit have been lifted, and those with spiritual eyes are able to understand these things with clarity. We thank you for your discipline when we err, love and blessings when we obey, and guidance to teach us how to be better prepared for our paths. We thank you for our thorns that prevent our boastfulness.

We ask for freedom from the chains of the world that keep us bound and prevent us from returning to a time of balance. We ask for further teaching on how to resurrect the land, waters, and air as it was in the beginning. May we return to such a time where we become the caretakers we were meant to be. There are so many innocents imprisoned unjustly, and we ask for their release from bondage. We ask that the veils of secrecy within government continue to open further so we may become better equipped to remedy man's willingness to succumb to greed, sexual perversion, and abuse of power. We ask for integrity and honor to enter the hearts and minds of those that lead. We ask for an end to the materialism, greed, hatred, and deceptive ways. We ask that the laws you've given are equal to all. There is so much violence going on in this world that our lives have become burdensome, and we ask for a time of peace and understanding. We ask for love to enter into the hearts of those that have chosen a life of hate, greed, and power. We ask for the protection of all the defenseless. We ask for your healing hands to guide those of surgeons this week that continue to operate on those in their operating rooms. We ask for healing for all that are suffering through diverse diseases and disorders. We also ask for healing for those that are despondent and low in spirit.

We thank you for the morning dew as it falls from the plants to the soil below. We thank you for the stillness of the lakes and ocean waters that bring us a calmness to our spirit. We thank you for the many herbs and plants that give us both nourishment and cures for all our diseases and ailments. We thank you for the remaining natural reserves that we can go to and regain our balance. *Emenv.*

GREAT SPIRIT, ALMIGHTY HEALER, and Creator of all things, it is with a humbled heart that we gather together to offer up many thanks. We thank you for the rising of the sun each morning as it brings warmth and light to our paths. We thank you for the rains that come to areas of great thirst. We thank you for the sacred circles found throughout your creation, from the vastness of the universe to the nests of the birds that surround us. We thank you for the seasonal circles that remind us of rejuvenation, growth, and rest within the cycle. We thank you for the music found in the winds and the rushing waters. We thank you for the moon as it watches over us during our slumber. We thank you for the sky as it displays the beauty of the golden hues in the morning and the reddish hues during the evening. We thank you for the earth as it supplies us with all we need to survive. We thank you for the lifeblood of all living things as it cascades down from the snowcapped mountains. We thank you for all the mysteries of the universe we behold. We thank you for the music we find in the early morning hours as the songbirds begin their songs.

We ask for strength, courage, and guidance for those that are now meeting their ancestors and loved ones in the spirit world. We ask for miraculous healing for those that are suffering from diverse diseases, ailments, and disorders. For those that are low in spirit, we ask for their comfort and guidance. We ask for protection, courage, and strength for all that will stand against the onslaught of destruction to our environment and animals by those that do not understand what they are doing. We ask for an end to the deep misunderstanding that seeks to divide your people. We ask for an end to the greed and lust of power that seeks to destroy the spirits of many. We ask for an era of peace and true equality where no one person has more power than the next. We ask for a return of our abducted sons and daughters and protect them from harm. We ask for guidance as we continue along our paths so we may choose the right direction. We ask for freedom for those that continue to suffer incarceration for crimes they did not commit. We ask for a greater compassion to soften the hardened hearts of those who do not understand the suffering of the homeless and the poor. We ask for a bountiful harvest so we may provide food for those that are starving throughout all four corners. We ask for a greater awakening and a cleansing of our spirits to prepare us for the arduous task of rebalancing that lies ahead. We ask for protection and courage also for those that will defend the defenseless. We ask for the hardened hearts of our enemies to be broken so they may come to find your glory. We ask for forgiveness, our country is divided by two factions: one for trying to bring your laws back into our lives, and the other for continuing to keep them out. We ask for your guidance and mercy, Father, as we begin to stand up for what is righteous.

We thank you for our elders and the wisdom of the ancestors they provide. We thank you for the life lessons they advise us of the present. We thank you for our children that remind us of lessons and innocence long forgotten. May we erect for them an unbreakable foundation to build upon for a brighter future. We thank you for all two-leggeds, four-leggeds, swimmers, fliers, and crawlers that interact with us and bring us insight and wisdom. We thank you for the strength of the wisdom that lies within our hearts. We thank you for the many trials we endure so they may strengthen our spirit and prepare us for the future. *Emenv.*

GREAT SPIRIT, ALMIGHTY HEALER, and Creator of all things, it is with humbled hearts that we gather together to offer many thanks. We thank you for the music of the crickets under the shadow of night, the howling of the wolf as he calls out to the moon, and the rushing waters of the falls deep in the forests. We thank you for the winds that flow through the blades of grass, and trees that blow out the old air to replace it with the new. We thank you for the early morning mist that floats down from above to provide the earth with moisture necessary for life. We thank you for all two-leggeds, four-leggeds, swimmers, fliers, and crawlers that we interact with each day. We thank you for the cool breeze of the early morning air as it gently caresses our cheek. For the signs and wonders of the heavens, we thank you. We thank you for the canopies of the willow, elm, and oak on a warm summer day.

    We ask for a growing spiritual revival that will soften even the hardest of hearts. We ask for eyes to open that have been closed for too long. May the veils of secrecy in all levels of government, corporations, and clubs continue to be lifted and exposed. Let us begin a life where no man is greater than the next and where nothing is done without the knowledge of your people. We ask for protection, courage, and strength to withstand the persecution that surrounds us. We ask for protection, strength, and great stamina for those that stand against the evil that continues to destroy your lands, animals, and cultures. We ask for our voices to be heard throughout the four corners where we can begin to teach those that are willing, your ways, and the tasks you have given us. We ask for an end to the hatred that has permeated throughout our society and bring peace to a land where we are suffering. We ask for true equality for all four colors where we are no longer controlled by greed or materialistic lust. We ask for an era of peace where we can once again unlock our doors without fear. We ask for an end to the man-made poisons created in the name of science and begin to rely upon the herbs and plants you have created for us. We ask for the return of our children that have been abducted. We ask for protection for our women and children that are suffering through violence and abuse. We ask for your forgiveness when we stray and your blessing when we have not. We ask for your healing hands to be placed upon those that are suffering through diverse diseases and disorders. For those that have lost loved ones, we ask for your comfort and peace be granted. We ask for strength, courage, and guidance for those that have gathered with their ancestors as they move into the next phase of life.

We thank you for our elders that have given us so much while we journeyed along our path. We thank you for our children that remind us of innocence and lessons long forgotten. We thank you for the nature that surrounds us and the tranquility it gives us when we take time out of our daily lives. We thank you for the many trials we encounter that serve to strengthen our spirit. We thank you for family and friends and the support they provide in times of need. We thank you for the precious gift of life. *Emenv.*

GREAT SPIRIT, ALMIGHTY HEALER, and Creator of all things, it is with a humbled heart that we gather together to offer up many thanks. We thank you for the many herbs and plants that provide us with cures for our ailments and diseases and for the nourishment that is given. We thank you for the waters that flow from the mountaintops that hydrate the bodies of all living things. We thank you for the trees and the rain forests that give us the air to breathe. We thank you for the gentle winds that soothes our spirits and the peacefulness it brings. We thank you for the tranquility that can be found in the nature surrounding us. We thank you for the wisdom found in the trees and animals that inhabit the forests. May we take the time to quiet ourselves, observe, and listen. We thank you for the early morning stillness of the lakes and oceans, reminding us that each day starts anew and many wondrous things can be accomplished. We thank you for the bad times as well as the good that show us that all things have their purpose. We thank you for those that comfort, cure, support, and defend us each day.

We ask for healing for those that are suffering through diverse diseases and disorders. We ask for your hands to be placed upon each surgeon's hands that will be operating in emergency rooms. We ask for comfort and guidance for those that are low in spirit. We ask for a great revival of spiritual awakening during this time of turmoil and distress. We ask for protection, guidance and strength as we stand against those that willfully destroy more of your creation. We ask for an end to the greed, corruption, lust of power and wealth that is found in our governments. We ask for an era of peace in a world that is weary of war and the governments that sanction them. We ask for the veils of secrecy to continue to be lifted so the people will begin to understand and make better informed decisions. We ask for a time where we can return our focus to you and allow your Word to, once again, enter the halls of our government and schools. We ask for an end to the violence and abuse being suffered by our women and children. We ask for closed eyes to open, hardened hearts to soften, and clogged ears to loosen in a time where unity of the four colors is needed. We ask for an end to the division that separates us and slows down the unity we need to bring back balance to this unbalanced world. We ask for the rains to come to areas of thirst. We ask for the awaited gathering of those that will begin to protect the animals from men that would hunt for sport and trophies. We ask for greater awareness and compassion toward those that are in need.

We thank you for our elders that bring us wisdom, life lessons, culture and heritage awareness, and the stories from long ago. We thank you for our children that will take the lessons and wisdom they learn from us on to the next generation. We thank you for the great expanse of the universe that surround us and is the very center of our being. We thank you for the wisdom and spirit that resides in the heart. We thank you for our ancestors that remain with us from the spirit world to help us during our journey. We thank you for those that protect and to serve your people each day amongst great sacrifice. We thank you for the knowledge that we are now at a point in our lives where we need to focus upon the spiritual battle we are now engaged with. We thank you for your forgiveness when we stray. We thank you for your love and guidance given to us each day. *Emenv.*

Great Spirit, Almighty Healer, and Creator of all things both seen and unseen, it is with humbled hearts that we come together as one to offer up many thanks. We thank you for the sacred circle of life that surrounds us. We thank you for the many plants and herbs that provide us with nutrition as well as for our cures. We thank you for the wisdom you have planted within our hearts and given us the knowledge that all things have a specific and unique purpose. We thank you for the teachings of our honorable elders. We thank you for our children that will continue these teachings on to the next generation. We thank you for the knowledge of the creation of the second heaven where you have placed the signs of your appointed times for us to watch for.

    We ask for your forgiveness, for we have done horrific things in your name that have caused much distress, harm, and genocide of peoples. We now live in a time where the people divide themselves by race, blood quantum, and religion, and we ask for a time where we consider only the character of a person. We ask for a cure for our addictions that prevent us from being the people we were meant to be. We ask for our lands to flourish once again. Many generations have passed, and the indigenous people that you have placed in the lands remain low in the eyes of governments and corporations. We ask for a time that you will raise them up to bring back the teachings and wisdom long forgotten. We ask for protection for all the defenseless, whether they be two-legged, four-legged, swimmers, fliers, or crawlers. We ask for an end to the destruction and pollution of the rainforests, dense forestlands, waters, and the air that we breathe. We ask for strength, courage, and peace to enter the hearts of our young ones who have been contemplating suicide. May they find their purpose and path in life to grab hold of its passion and to move forward with straight eyes and strong legs. We ask for peace and the return of our children from across the great waters. Grant them protection and bless them, Father.

We thank you for each new dawn that promises us another day of life. We thank you for the air we breathe, the water we drink, and the food we eat. We ask for your blessing upon our meals. We thank you for granting us the necessities of life. May we become more compassionate and ensure these things are given to those in need. We thank you for your love, forgiveness, mercy, and guidance. *Emenv.*

GREAT SPIRIT, ALMIGHTY HEALER, and Creator of all things, it is with humbled hearts that we unite together to offer up many thanks. We thank you for the spirit that dwells within us and in all living things. We thank you for our ancestors that are still with us in spirit and the wisdom they provide. We thank you for all two-leggeds, four-leggeds, swimmers, fliers, and crawlers that surround us. We thank you for the music found in the gentle winds that flow through the trees and the cascading waters. We thank you for the trials we endure that strengthen and prepare us for what lies ahead. We thank you for the many answered prayers.

We ask for your healing hands to be placed upon those that are suffering from man-made and natural diseases and disorders. We ask for a greater awakening during this time so we may begin the long struggle of bringing back balance. We ask for an end to the turmoil that has kept your people divided for too long so we may work toward balance. We ask for an end to such hatred, greed, lust of power and materialism that is found in our governments and corporations that have filled the hearts of those that have become complacent and naive. We ask for freedom for those that have been abducted or taken from their homes without cause. We ask for protection for your forests, waters, plains, and deserts that man has taken parts of your creation without replacing. We ask for strength, guidance, and courage for those that stand against governments that do not protect the lands or the treaties they have signed. Where there may be wildfires, we ask for rains to come to help in squelching them. We ask for protection for all two-leggeds, four-leggeds, swimmers, fliers, and crawlers that are facing grave danger. May we be of strong heart and defend all that are defenseless. We ask for guidance each day so we may travel our paths with courage, strong legs, and straight eyes. We ask for more compassion to be placed upon the hearts of those that are aware of the homeless in their cities. We ask for more open doors for them so they may once again be able to live productive lives.

We thank you for our elders that show us many life lessons and wisdom to carry within us during our journey. May we always endeavor to bring great honor to them. We thank you for our children that continue to teach us innocence and lessons long forgotten. May we provide them with an unbreakable foundation from which they will build on. We thank you for our relations that interact with us during the day that strengthen our spirits. We thank you for the gift of life and the paths you have given us. May we learn to listen intently before we speak and understand that there is strength in silence. *Emenv.*

GREAT SPIRIT, ALMIGHTY HEALER, and Creator of all things seen and unseen, it is with humbled hearts that we unite together as one to offer up many thanks. We thank you for your love and guidance when we do right, your discipline when we are wrong, and your thoughtfulness to stay with us when we look to you. We thank you for the answering all of our prayers each day. We thank you for our daily food and ask for its blessing. We thank you for the knowledge you impart to us through the Sacred Spirit and the insights we receive from others along our path.

We ask for patience, strength, and guidance in the proper rearing of our children. We ask for a time of tranquility, apart from worldly matters, so we may concentrate on your blessings and guidance. We ask for protection for those going through severe storms, fires, earthquakes, and floods. We ask for your hands to guide those of the surgeons that are performing operations. For those that are suffering through the many various diseases and disorders, we ask for your healing hands to be placed upon them. We ask for calm in a world filled with anger and hatred and understanding that all lives matter within the human circle. We ask for truth and clarity from those that bring us your Word and instruction on how we should be living our lives. We ask for greater compassion to enter the hearts and minds of all people not just during disasters, but daily. We ask for protection for our women and children from violence and abuse. We ask for rain for the areas going through severe droughts and wildfires.

We thank you for our elders that bring us wisdom, guidance, and spiritual healing. We thank you for our children that will take these things and teach them to the next generation. We thank you for the earth's lifeblood that brings growth and hydration to all living things. We thank you for the trees that take our carbon dioxide and create oxygen for us to breathe. We thank you for all two-leggeds, four-leggeds, swimmers, fliers, and crawlers. We thank you for still waters and plush forests. *Emenv.*

GREAT SPIRIT, ALMIGHTY HEALER, and Creator of all things, it is with humbled hearts that we gather together to offer many thanks. We thank you for the music of the crickets under the shadow of night, the howling of the wolf as he calls out to the moon, and the rushing waters of the falls deep in the forests. We thank you for the winds that flow through the blades of grass and trees that blow out the old air to replace it with the new. We thank you for the early morning mist that floats down from above to provide the earth with moisture necessary for life. We thank you for all two-leggeds, four-leggeds, swimmers, fliers, and crawlers that we interact with each day. We thank you for the cool breeze of the early morning air as it gently caresses our cheek. We thank you for the sounds of the seagulls flying over the ocean waters of the shore.

We ask for a growing spiritual revival that will soften even the hardest of hearts. We ask for eyes to open that have been closed for too long. May the veils of secrecy in all levels of government, corporations and clubs be lifted and exposed. Let us begin a life where no man is greater than the next and where nothing is done without the knowledge of your people. We ask for protection, courage, and strength to withstand the persecution that surrounds us from terrorists, antifa, and others that seek to harm others for the sake of globalism. We ask for protection, strength, and great stamina for those that stand against the evil that continues to destroy your lands, animals, and cultures. We ask for our voices to be heard throughout the four corners where we can begin to teach those that are willing, your ways, and the tasks you have given us. We ask for an end to the hatred that has permeated throughout our society and bring peace to a land where we are suffering. We ask for true equality for all four colors where we are no longer controlled by greed or materialistic lust. We ask for an era of peace where we can once again unlock our doors without fear. We ask for an end to the man-made poisons created in the name of science and begin to rely upon the herbs and plants you have created for us. We ask for the return of our children that have been abducted. We ask for protection for our women and children that are suffering through violence and abuse. We ask for your forgiveness when we stray and your blessing when we have not. We ask for freedom for those that have been incarcerated for crimes they did not commit. We ask for your healing hands to be placed upon those that are suffering through diverse diseases and disorders. For those that have lost loved ones, we ask for your comfort and peace be granted. We ask for strength, courage, and guidance for those that have gathered with their ancestors as they move into the next phase of life.

We thank you for our elders that have given us so much while we journeyed along our path. We thank you for our children that remind us of innocence and lessons long forgotten. We thank you for the nature that surrounds us and the tranquility it gives when we take time out of our daily lives. We thank you for the many trials we encounter that serve to strengthen our spirit. We thank you for family and friends and the support they provide in times of need. We thank you for the precious gift of life. *Emenv.*

GREAT SPIRIT, ALMIGHTY HEALER, and Creator of all things, we united together with humbled hearts to offer up many thanks. We thank you for the rising of the sun as it lights up our path and provides warmth. We thank you for the moon as it watches over us during our slumber. We thank you for the sky that protects us each day and night. We thank you for our earth that supplies us with all that we need to survive. We thank you for the gift of life; you have breathed in to every living thing. We thank you for the many blessings and gifts you have given us. We thank you for all two-leggeds, four-leggeds, swimmers, fliers, and crawlers that we may interact with each day. We thank you for each new sunrise that reminds us of the gift of each new day granted. We thank you for the beauty of the sunset with its hues of red, orange, and yellow.

We have allowed materialistic greed and money to control us. We ask for your forgiveness and guidance toward returning to a time when we were better caretakers of your creation. We have polluted the lands, waters, and sky and have brought hatred, corruption, and division where we were once united in peace. We ask for a return to an era of peace where all people are truly equal, and we use the gifts provided to bring back balance to a world that is destroying itself. We ask for protection for our animal brothers and sisters that are facing grave danger from men that have lost all understanding and love of life. We ask for protection for the women and children that continue to suffer through violence and abuse. We ask for strength, guidance, and courage as we stand against those that would continue to destroy the lands, waters, and skies above. We ask for an end to the corruption, greed, and lust of power and wealth of those that are supposed to serve their people. We ask for an end to the division that continues to keep your people from uniting and fulfilling the prophecies. We ask for the release of all your children that have been incarcerated for crimes they did not commit. We ask for a time for boys to become men and become real fathers to the children they have sired. We ask for hardened hearts to soften and compassion be used to help the poor, homeless, widows, and all that are in need. We ask for guidance each day so we may work toward an era of renewal and heal our earth. We ask for protection for all that are defenseless against the onslaught of evil that surrounds them. We are with heavy hearts and are weary of such mindless aggression and wish only unity and balance in an unbalanced world. We ask for a greater spiritual awakening in hearts that have been bound by stereotype and racist views for too long. We ask for the return of our children that have been missing from their families.

We thank you for our many trials as they bring strength to our spirits. We thank you for our elders as they bring us the instruction and wisdom needed to follow our path. We thank you for our children that will build upon the foundation we have set before them. We thank you for our relations that interact with us each day to give us insight in areas of misunderstanding. We thank you for our family and friends that give us the support we need along our journey. *Emenv.*

GREAT SPIRIT, ALMIGHTY HEALER, and Creator of all things, it is with a humbled heart that we gather together to offer up many thanks. We thank you for the rains that come to areas of great thirst. We thank you for the sacred circles found throughout your creation, from the vastness of the universe to the nests of the birds that surround us. We thank you for the seasonal circles that remind us of rejuvenation, growth, and rest within the cycle. We thank you for the music found in the winds and the rushing waters. We thank you for the fruit of the vine, bush, and tree. We thank you for all the mysteries of the universe we behold. We thank you for the music we find in the early morning hours as the songbirds begin their songs. We thank you for the beauty of the butterfly as it emerges from its cocoon. We thank you for the sight of the dragonfly skimming across the pond. We thank you for the hummingbird hovering over the flower as it prepares to receive its nectar.

We ask for strength, courage, and guidance for those that are now meeting their ancestors and loved ones in the spirit world. We ask for miraculous healing for those that are suffering from diverse diseases and disorders. For those that are low in spirit, we ask for their comfort and guidance. We ask for protection, courage, and strength for all that will stand against the onslaught of destruction to our environment and animals by those that do not understand what they are doing. We ask for an end to the hatred that seeks to divide your people. We ask for an end to the greed and lust of power that seeks to destroy the spirits of many. We ask for the return of our abducted sons and daughters and protect them from harm. We ask for guidance as we continue along our paths so we may choose the right direction. We ask for freedom for those that continue to suffer incarceration for crimes they did not commit. We ask for a greater compassion to soften the hardened hearts who do not understand the suffering of the homeless and the poor. We ask for a bountiful harvest so we may provide food for those that are starving throughout all four corners. We ask for a greater awakening and a cleansing of our spirits to prepare us for the arduous task of rebalancing that lies ahead. We ask for protection of our animal friends that are facing grave danger from those that would kill them for trophies. We ask for protection also for those that stand against the onslaught of evil. We ask for a regeneration of the environment and for a strong unity among the four corners. We ask for protection, strength, and courage also for those that will defend the defenseless. We ask for the hardened hearts of our enemies to be broken so they may come to find your glory. We ask for your mercy, Father, as we begin to stand up for what is righteous while we await your return. We continue to ask for the protection, strength, and guidance for the president and his family. We ask for protection and strength for our servicemen and women as well.

We thank you for our elders and the wisdom of the ancestors they provide. We thank you for the life lessons they advise us of the present. We thank you for our children that remind us of lessons and innocence long forgotten. May we erect for them an unbreakable foundation to build upon for a brighter future. We thank you for all two-leggeds, four-leggeds, swimmers, fliers, and crawlers that interact with us and bring us insight and wisdom. We thank you for the strength of the wisdom that lies within our hearts. We thank you for the many trials we endure so they may strengthen our spirit and prepare us for the future. *Emenv.*

GREAT SPIRIT, ALMIGHTY HEALER, and Creator of all things, it is with a humbled heart that we unite together to offer up many thanks. We thank you for the precious gift of life. We thank you for our elders that give us the instruction and the wisdom we need along our path. We thank you for our children that bring us reminders of innocence and lessons lost long ago. We thank you for our relations that may come and go but bring us insight along the way. We thank you for the wisdom you have instilled within our hearts. For the many blessings you have bestowed upon us, we thank you. We thank you for this period of the awakening of spirits that bring those assimilated to learn more of their culture.

We ask for greater awareness of how precious life is and how it should be allowed to blossom. We ask for an end to the hatred that continues to divide us. We ask for protection, strength, and courage as we face those that continue to destroy the environment and the animals that live there. We ask for a time where our weariness of war, greed, lust of power and wealth is replaced with a more peaceful, spiritual life. We ask for protection of the defenseless and the innocent throughout the four corners that are facing hostilities. We ask for greater clarity and the continual lifting of the veils of secrecy. We ask for hope for the hopeless and more compassion toward those that are struggling to survive. We ask for your healing hands to be placed upon those that are suffering through diverse diseases and disorders. We ask for an era of global revitalization where we are able to replenish the forests and plains, the cleaning of our air and waters, cleanliness of our planetary orbit. We ask for your forgiveness when we stray. We ask for an end to the wanton killing of our brothers the bear, wolf, horse, buffalo, whale, and dolphin for trophies or sport.

We ask for a time where all people are truly equal where no one person is greater than the next so we may be able to unite together as one to reclaim your lands and be better stewards than we have been. We ask for protection, strength, and guidance for those that stand up for the defenseless. We ask for the answer to questions for the young that are seeking truth. We ask for clarity and guidance during this time or turmoil so we may begin to understand the paths you have placed before us.

We thank you for the rain forests that provide us with the air to breathe. We thank you for the waters that flow from the mountaintops that hydrate us. We thank you for our daily food and ask for its blessing. We thank you for your spirit that resides in us all. We thank you for the peace and wisdom that can be found in nature when we are able to take the time to connect. We thank you for the sun as it rises each morning and the moon as it watches over us during our slumber. We thank you for the sky as it protects us throughout the day and night. We thank you for this earth for all that it provides us to survive. *Emenv.*

GREAT SPIRIT, ALMIGHTY HEALER, and Creator of all things, we gather together this day with humbled hearts to offer up many thanks. We thank you for all two-leggeds, four-leggeds, swimmers, fliers, and crawlers. We thank you for the wisdom found in nature and through the many experiences we have faced along our journey. We thank you for the music found in the gentle winds and the rushing waters. We thank you for the howls of the coyotes of the desert and the wolves of the forests and mountains. We thank you for the strength shown in the soaring of the eagle in the north and the hawk in the south. We thank you for the gift of life and the many blessings you have bestowed upon your children. We thank you for the fragrance of the lilac and the lavender.

We ask for those with hardened hearts to be allowed to see the destruction they have caused over the years. We ask for an end to the division among the people so they may see the deception placed upon them by the elite forces. We ask for an end to the hatred and racism that divides us from our brothers and sisters. We ask for an end to the greed that permeates throughout the four corners and the lust of materialistic desires be laid waste. We ask for an end to all hostilities in a world where the people are war-weary. We ask instead for an era of peace among all nations. We ask for your miraculous healing hands to be placed upon those that are suffering through physical and mental diseases and disorders. We ask for your hands to guide surgeons as they operate on those in operating rooms this day. We ask for protection for those that continue to stand against governments and corporations that would take away their culture and further destroy all that you have created. For those that have lost loved ones, we ask for comfort for them during their grieving process. We ask for strength, courage, and guidance be given to those that are now in the spirit world. We ask for protection from those that wish only to bring harm to us and our way of life.

We thank you for our elders and the lessons they teach us today as well as the wisdom of the ancestors. May we honor them with the deepest respect. We thank you for our children that remind us of the innocence and the lessons we have long forgotten. May we continue to strengthen the foundation set forth by the seventh generation so they may have an unbreakable foundation to build upon. We thank you for our daily food and the waters that hydrate us. We thank you for the rain forests that provide us with the air to breathe. We thank you for the vast oceans that give us the moisture for the clouds that give us the rains that are needed. We thank you for your love and your forgiveness when we stray from our path. *Emenv.*

GREAT SPIRIT, ALMIGHTY HEALER, and Creator of all things, we gather together this day with humbled hearts to offer up many thanks. We thank you for all two-leggeds, four-leggeds, swimmers, fliers, and crawlers. We thank you for the wisdom found in nature and through the many experiences we have faced along our journey. We thank you for the swaying of the palms along the shore as the tropical winds flow along the sandy beach. We thank you for the coconuts that fall from the palm and provide us with its savory water.

We ask for a brief pause during this time of revival to bring forth a purification of our souls. We ask for those with hardened hearts to be allowed to see the destruction they have caused over the years. We ask for all veils of secrecy to be lifted where nothing is ever again allowed to happen without the knowledge of the people. We ask for justice for the victims of horrendous crimes. We ask for an end to the hatred that divides us from our brothers and sisters. We ask for an end to the greed that permeates throughout the four corners and the lust of materialistic desires be laid waste. We ask for true equality where no one person is more powerful than the next. We ask for an end to all hostilities and wars in a world where the people are war-weary. We ask instead for an era of peace among all nations. We ask for your miraculous healing hands to be placed upon those that are suffering through physical and mental diseases and disorders. We ask for your hands to guide surgeons as they operate on those in operating rooms this day. We ask for protection for those that continue to stand against governments and corporations that would take away their culture and further destroy all that you have created. We ask for protection of our brothers the wolf, bear, buffalo, horse, whale, and dolphin and for those that are defenseless. For those that have lost loved ones, we ask for comfort be granted them. We ask for strength, courage, and guidance be given to those that are now in the spirit world. We ask for protection from those that wish only to bring harm to us and our way of life. We pray that they will come to find you and place you within their hearts.

We thank you for our elders and the lessons they teach us today as well as the wisdom of the ancestors. May we honor them with the deepest respect. We thank you for our children that remind us of the innocence and the lessons we have long forgotten. May we continue to strengthen the foundation set forth by the seventh generation so they may have an unbreakable foundation to build upon. We thank you for our daily food and the waters that hydrate us. We thank you for the rain forests that provide us with the air to breathe. We thank you for the vast oceans that give us the moisture for the clouds that give us the rains that are needed. We thank you for your love and your forgiveness when we stray from our path. *Emenv.*

GREAT SPIRIT, ALMIGHTY HEALER, and Creator of all things, with humbled hearts we unite together to offer up many thanks. We thank you for the gentle winds as they flow through the trees and the grassy plains. We thank you for the waters that flow from the snowcapped mountains to the oceans below. We thank you for all two-leggeds, four-leggeds, swimmers, fliers, and crawlers that inhabit the earth. We thank you for the clouds that carry the rains from the oceans to areas that have become arid. We thank you for our daily food and ask for its blessing. We thank you for the music from the crickets under the shadow of night and the fliers that wake us in the early morning hours. We thank you for the beauty of the dancing fireflies in the early evening hours. For the strength and the persistence of the eagle, we thank you. We thank you for the farmers that grow the grains and vegetables that ultimately feed the hungry.

We ask for an end to homelessness and for closed doors of opportunity to open. We ask for a bountiful harvest in the coming year so all people can be fed. We ask for an end to famine and disease. We ask for compassion toward the poor who face devastatingly cold winters. May they receive the necessary blankets, clothing, and food for their families. We ask for your healing hands to be placed upon those suffering through diverse diseases, disorders, and ailments. For those that have lost loved ones, we ask for comfort and peace be granted during their time of grievance. For those imprisoned for crimes they did not commit, we ask for their release. We ask for an end to the violence and abuse being suffered by our women and children. We ask for forgiveness, Father, for we have caused great destruction to our earth through pollution, litter, mining, flacking, and strip mining; we have cut down trees without replanting, poisoned our air, and hunted for sport and trophies. We ask for hardened hearts to soften, closed eyes to open, clogged ears to hear. We ask for veils of secrecy throughout the four corners to continue to be lifted. We ask for protection, guidance, and strength as we stand against injustice and against those that would willingly bring more destruction to your creation. We ask for the changing of mindsets in our government so they may begin to return to a time where our focus was upon you and your blessings. We ask for greater compassion toward the unborn. We ask for your protection and guidance to be over those leading our country and are trying to turn our focus back toward you. We ask for guidance and protection to be granted to our president and his family as well as for all godly people.

We thank you for our elders that deserve so much respect. May we teach our children the importance of respecting all things especially those of our elders. We thank you for our children that continue to remind us of lessons long forgotten. We thank you for our earth, the sky, the sun, and the moon. We thank you for the precious gift of life and the unique paths given. We thank you for your love, forgiveness, correction, and patience. *Emenv.*

GREAT SPIRIT, ALMIGHTY HEALER, and Creator of all things seen and unseen, it is with humbled hearts that we unite together as one to offer up many thanks. We thank you for your love and guidance when we do right, your discipline when we are wrong, and your thoughtfulness to stay with us as we look to you. We thank you for the answering of our prayers each day. We thank you for our daily food and ask for its blessing. We thank you for the knowledge you impart to us through the Sacred Spirit and the insights we receive from others along our path.

We ask for patience, strength, and guidance in the proper rearing of our children. We ask for a time of tranquility, apart from worldly matters, so we may concentrate on your blessings and guidance. We ask for protection for those going through severe storms, earthquakes, fires, and floods. We ask for your hands to guide those of the surgeons that are performing operations. For those that are suffering through the many various diseases and disorders, we ask for your healing hands to be placed upon them. We ask for calm in a world filled with anger and hatred. We ask for truth and clarity from those that bring us your Word and instruction on how we should be living our lives. We ask for greater compassion to enter the hearts and minds of all people. We ask for protection for our women and children from violence and abuse. We ask for the release of all innocent political prisoners and bring them home to their families and friends.

We thank you for our elders that bring us wisdom, guidance, and spiritual healing. We thank you for our children that will take these things and teach them to the next generation. We thank you for the earth's lifeblood that brings growth and hydration to all living things. We thank you for the trees that take our carbon dioxide and create oxygen for us to breathe. We thank you for all two-leggeds, four-leggeds, swimmers, fliers, crawlers, and rock people. We thank you for still waters and plush forests. We thank you for lessons learned through the observation of nature. *Emenv.*

GREAT SPIRIT, ALMIGHTY HEALER, and Creator of all things, it is with a humbled heart that we gather together to offer up many thanks. We thank you for the warmth of the sun during the day and the coolness of the moon at night. We thank you for the many herbs and plants that provide us with cures for our ailments and diseases and for the nourishment that is given. We thank you for the waters that flow from the mountaintops that hydrate the bodies of all living things. We thank you for the trees and the rain forests that give us the air to breathe. We thank you for the gentle winds that soothes our spirits. We thank you for the peace that can be found in the nature that surrounds us. We thank you for the sacred circle that can be found throughout your creation, from the vastness of the universe around us to the very core of our earth.

We ask for healing for those that are suffering through diverse diseases and disorders. We ask for your hands to be placed upon the surgeon's hands that will be operating in emergency rooms this day. We ask for comfort and guidance for those that are low in spirit. We ask for a great revival of spiritual awakening during this time of turmoil and distress. We ask for protection for our animal friends, the bear, the wolf, the horse, the buffalo, the whale, and the dolphin that are facing grave danger from those that do not understand how precious all life is. We ask for protection, guidance, and strength as we stand against those that willfully destroy more of your creation. We ask for an era of peace in a world that is weary of war and the governments that sanction them. We ask for an end to the violence and abuse being suffered by our women and children. We ask for closed eyes to open, hardened hearts to soften, and clogged ears to loosen in a time where unity of the four colors is needed. We ask for an end to the division that separates us and slows down the togetherness we need to bring back balance to an unbalanced world. We ask for your guidance and direction to enter the halls of our governments and an end to the corruption that has transplanted itself throughout the years. We ask for the remnant of your people to wax great during these last days. We ask for your guidance, courage, and truth to be shown through our example and our speech.

We thank you for our elders that bring us wisdom, life lessons, culture, heritage awareness, and the stories from long ago. We thank you for our children that will take the lessons and wisdom they learn from us and bring them to the next generation. We thank you for the wisdom and spirit that resides in the heart. We thank you for our ancestors that remain with us from the spirit world to help us during our journey. We thank you for your forgiveness when we stray. We thank you for your love and guidance given to us each day. We thank you for the many gifts and blessings you have bestowed upon us. We thank you for all answered prayers. *Emenv.*

GREAT SPIRIT, ALMIGHTY HEALER, and Creator of all things, with humbled hearts we gather together to offer up many thanks. We thank you for the four seasons and the understanding that they too serve a purpose. We thank you for the mists that float down into the valleys below to bring moisture to the soil. We thank you for the clouds that bring the rain to areas of thirst. We thank you for the music found among the crawlers and fliers under the evening sky. We thank you for the coolness of the morning air and the gentle breeze that brush across our cheeks. We thank you for the winds that rid us of the old air and bring in the new. We thank you for the beauty of the butterfly to the swiftness of the dragonfly. We thank you for the songs of the songbirds in the early morning hours. We thank you for the bees that bring pollination to the plants.

We ask for healing across the four corners for all that are suffering through diverse diseases, disorders, and ailments. We ask for strength, courage, and guidance for those now meeting their ancestors. We ask for comfort and guidance for those that have lost their way or are low in spirit. For those threatened by natural disasters, we ask for their protection. We ask also for the protection of our brothers—the animals that inhabit the forests, plains, deserts, and oceans. For those that stand against further destruction of your creation, we ask for their protection; grant them courage and strength so they may stand against any obstacle towards returning balance to the environment. We ask for mercy toward those that do not understand the wrongful actions they have taken. We ask for hardened hearts to soften, closed minds to open, blind eyes to see, and clogged ears to hear. Bring them understanding that all they have been taught may not be truth. We ask for an end to modern-day slavery and the return of our children. We continue to be weary of war and hostilities conducted by those that bring about evil and greed. We ask for an era of peace where all people are united together and are truly equal, where no person is more powerful than the next. We ask for a resurgence of the divine spirit across the four corners and the four colors so we may begin to right the wrongs of the past and present. We ask for protection for our women and children that continue to be abused.

We thank you, Almighty Father, for our elders that continue to teach us what we need to understand during this time of turmoil. We thank you for our children that continue to show us lessons we have long forgotten. We thank you for our daily food and ask for its blessing. We thank you for the rushing waters flowing from snow-capped mountains to hydrate us. We thank you for the many herbs and plants that both nourish and cure us. We thank you for family and friends that support us along our path. We thank you for the many blessings and gifts you have bestowed upon us. May we use them as you intended. We thank you for your love, forgiveness, patience, and guidance. We thank you for the precious gift of life and the knowledge that all things are sacred. *Emenv.*

GREAT SPIRIT, ALMIGHTY HEALER, and Creator of all things, with humbled hearts, we gather together to offer up many thanks. We thank you for the four seasons and the understanding that they too serve a purpose. We thank you for the rising of the sun from the east that brings warmth and light. We thank you for the mists that float down into the valleys below to bring moisture to the soil. We thank you for the clouds that bring the rain to areas of thirst. We thank you for the moon as it watches over us during our slumber. We thank you for the music found among the crawlers and fliers under the shadow of night. We thank you for the surrounding sky that protects us from the radioactive particles from space. We thank you for our earth that sustains us with all we need to survive. We thank you for the coolness of the morning air and the breeze that gently caresses across our cheeks. We thank you for the winds that rid us of the old air and replaces it with the new.

We ask for strength, courage, and guidance for those now meeting their ancestors. We ask for comfort and guidance for those that have lost their way or are low in spirit. For those threatened by fires, floods, and earthquakes, we ask for their protection. We ask also for the protection of our brothers—the animals that inhabit the forests, plains, deserts, and oceans. For those that stand against further destruction of your creation, we ask for their protection; grant them courage and strength so they may stand against any obstacle towards returning balance to the environment. We ask for mercy toward those that do not understand the wrongful actions they have taken. We ask for hardened hearts to soften, closed minds to open, blind eyes to see, and clogged ears to hear. Bring them understanding that all they have been taught may not be truth. We ask for an end to modern-day slavery and the return of our children. We continue to be weary of war and hostilities conducted by those that bring about evil and greed. We ask for an era of peace where all people are united together and are truly equal, where no person is more powerful than the next. We ask for the release of all political prisoners and those wrongfully convicted of crimes they did not do. We ask for a resurgence of the divine spirit across the four corners and the four colors so we may begin to right the wrongs of the past and present. We ask for protection for our women and children that continue to be abused. May our thoughts and focus be upon you rather than the world. We ask that you have mercy upon those that seek you, and may you bring more into your fold.

We thank you, Almighty Father, for our elders that continue to teach us what we need to understand during this time of turmoil. We thank you for our children that continue to show us lessons we have long forgotten. We thank you for our daily food and ask for its blessing. We thank you for the rushing waters flowing from snow-capped mountains to hydrate us. We thank you for the many herbs and plants that both nourish and cure us. We thank you for family and friends that support us along our path. We thank you for the many blessings and gifts you have bestowed upon us. May we use them as you intended. We thank you for your love, forgiveness, patience, and guidance. We thank you for the precious gift of life and the knowledge that all things are sacred. *Emenv.*

GREAT SPIRIT, ALMIGHTY HEALER, and Creator of all things both seen and unseen, it is with humbled hearts that we come together as one to offer up many thanks. We thank you for the sacred circle of life that surrounds us. We thank you for the many plants and herbs that provide us with nutrition as well as for our cures. We thank you for the wisdom you have planted within our hearts and given us the knowledge that all things have a specific and unique purpose. We thank you for the teachings of our honorable elders. We thank you for our children that will continue these teachings on to the next generation. We thank you for the knowledge of the creation of the second heaven where you have placed the signs of your appointed times for us to watch for.

We ask for your forgiveness, for we have done horrific things in your name that have caused much distress, harm, and genocide of peoples. We now live in a time where the people divide themselves by race, blood quantum, and religion, and we ask for a time where we consider only the character of a person. We ask for a cure for our addictions that prevent us from being the people we were meant to be. We ask for our lands to flourish once again. Many generations have passed, and the indigenous people that you have placed in the lands remain low in the eyes of governments and corporations. We ask for a time that you will raise them up and bring back the teachings and wisdom long forgotten. We ask for protection for all the defenseless whether they be two-legged, four-legged, swimmers, fliers, or crawlers. We ask for an end to the destruction and pollution of the rain forests, dense forestlands, waters, and the air that we breathe. We ask for strength, courage, and peace to enter the hearts of our young ones who have been contemplating suicide. May they find their purpose and path in life, to grab hold of its passion, and to move forward with straight eyes and strong legs. We ask for peace and the return of our children from across the great waters. Grant them protection and bless them, Father.

We thank you for each new dawn that promises us another day of life. We thank you for this precious gift. We thank you for the air we breathe, the water we drink, and the food we eat. We ask for your blessing upon our meals. We thank you for granting us the necessities of life. May we become more compassionate and ensure these things are given to those in need. We thank you for your love, forgiveness, mercy, and guidance. *Emenv.*

GREAT SPIRIT, ALMIGHTY HEALER, and Creator of all things, it is with a humbled heart that we come together to offer up many thanks. There is so much to be thankful for that it is difficult to be able to name them all in one prayer. For the beauty we see when we are in nature and the insight we receive, we thank you. We thank you for the rains that come to arid areas when we pray for your assistance. We thank you for the precious gift of life and the guidance you give us along our path. We thank you for our daily food, air to breathe, and waters that hydrate all living things. We thank you for the gentle breeze during the early morning hours that caress our cheeks.

We ask for your comfort, healing, and courage to be given to those that were harmed in senseless shootings in gang-infested areas. For those that were killed, we ask for their guidance and comfort in the next phase of life. For their families, we ask for comfort and strength during their grieving process. We ask also for your healing hands to be placed upon those suffering through diverse diseases and disorders. We ask for an era without violence where people can come together and begin to understand each other. We ask for protection for all that are defenseless. We ask for clarity of the understanding of our paths. For those that are low in spirit, we ask for your guidance, comfort, and courage afforded to them. We ask for your mercy when we have done wrong and blessings when you find favor with us. We ask for a world of peace and tranquility where all people work together without fear of the hatred we are surrounded with in the present. We ask for integrity and honor to enter the hearts and minds of those that rule over their citizenry. We ask for a time of great spiritual revival in this tumultuous time.

We thank you for the many herbs and plants that will provide us with all we need for our many ailments, disorders, and diseases. Thank you for the knowledge that you have provided everything we need to cure us, if only we would begin to understand. We thank you for those that bring us insight when we are in need. For those that provide aid and comfort for the poor, widows, children, and homeless, we thank you. We thank you for your unwavering love and forgiveness. May we all strive to be more like you rather than follow the world like blind sheep without a shepherd. *Emenv.*

Great Spirit, Almighty Healer, and Creator of all things, it is with humbled hearts that we unite together to offer up many thanks. We thank you for our ancestors that are still with us in spirit and the wisdom they bring. We thank you for all two-leggeds, four-leggeds, swimmers, fliers, and crawlers that surround us each day. We thank you for the music found in the gentle winds that flow through the trees and cascading waters. We thank you for the trials we endure to strengthen us and prepare us for what lies ahead. We thank you for the many answered prayers. We thank you for our daily food and ask for its blessing. We thank you for the waters that flow from the snowcapped mountains to the lakes and rivers below, bringing us the hydration our bodies need. We thank you for the trees and plants of the rain forests that provide us with the air to breathe. We thank you for the diverse fruits on the tree, bush, and the vine.

We ask for your healing hands to be placed upon those that are suffering from man-made and natural diseases and disorders. We ask for a greater awakening of our soul during this time so we may begin the long struggle of bringing back balance. We ask for an end to the turmoil that has kept your people divided for too long. We ask for freedom for those that have been abducted or taken from their homes without just cause. We ask for protection for your jungles, forests, waters, plains, and deserts that man has taken parts of your creation without replacing. We ask for strength, guidance, and courage for those that stand against governments that do not protect the lands or the treaties they have signed. We ask for calm in our streets from those that willfully set out to destroy rather than bringing about peaceful protests. We ask for protection for all two-leggeds, four-leggeds, swimmers, fliers, and crawlers that are facing grave danger.

May we be of strong heart and defend all that are defenseless. We ask for guidance each day so we may travel our paths with courage, strong legs, and straight eyes. We ask for more compassion to be placed upon the hearts of those that are aware of the homeless in their cities. We ask for more open doors for them so they may once again be able to live productive lives. We ask for your guidance to our leaders so they may make righteous decisions for their people. We ask for protection for Israel as well as for those that govern us. We ask for an end to the corruption within the three branches of government—wherever they may be.

We thank you for our elders that show us many life lessons and wisdom to carry within us during our journey. May we always endeavor to bring great honor to them. We thank you for our children that continue to teach us innocence and lessons long forgotten. May we provide them with an unbreakable foundation from which they will build on. We thank you for our relations that interact with us during the day that strengthen our spirits. We thank you for the gift of life and the paths you have given us. We thank you for the wisdom of the heart. May we learn to listen intently before we speak and understand the strength found in silence. *Emenv.*

GREAT SPIRIT, ALMIGHTY HEALER, and Creator of all things, with humbled hearts, we gather together to offer up many thanks. We thank you for the gift of life and the blessings you have given to your children. We thank you for the majestic mountains to the calmness of the oceans during the early morning hours. We thank you for the music found in the winds and rushing waters when we take the time to listen. We thank you for the mists floating down in the morning hours that bring nourishment to the thirsty plant life and the waters that hydrate all two-leggeds, four-leggeds, swimmers, fliers, and crawlers. We thank you for the precious gift of life and the sacredness of your creation. We thank you for the beauty of the bee as it pollinates the flower and the hovering of the hummingbird as it gathers its nectar. We thank you for the fruit of the tree and vine that brings us nourishment. We thank you for the fluttering of both the butterfly and dragonfly as they glide through the air.

We ask for greater patience so we are slow to anger during this day. We ask for greater humility when we tend to be boastful. We ask for greater tolerance when we tend to become angry or disagreeable to others. We ask for unity when we are divided. We ask for healing for those that are suffering through diverse diseases and disorders. We ask for your guidance and strength to be given to those that are low in spirit. We ask for a time of peace in a world filled with violence and division. We ask for truth during a time of great deception. We ask for a time where trust and honesty become commonplace. We ask for strength of will when we travel along our paths and that our eyes remain straight. We ask for an end to the violence and abuse being suffered by our women and children. We ask for an end to homelessness. We ask for greater compassion where we do not focus on ourselves as much as we should our brothers and sisters. We ask for the return of our children and women that have been abducted. We ask for an end to war and the return of our sons and daughters. We continue to ask for freedom for those that have been unjustly imprisoned under falsehoods and deceit. We ask for the cleansing of our hearts so we may better understand the messages sent. We ask for the cleansing of our feet so we may travel our paths tirelessly. We ask for the cleansing of our eyes, so we may see the many signs and wonders of this world. We ask for the cleansing of our hands so we may create beautiful things. We ask for the cleansing of our throats so we may speak rightly when words are needed. We ask for the cleansing of our ears so we may hear your guidance more clearly.

We thank you for the sky that continues to protect us throughout the day. We thank you for the earth, although ailing from our abuse, still provides us with the cures and nutrition we need to survive. We thank you for the rain forests that provide us with the air to breathe. We thank you for the rushing waters from the mountains that continue to hydrate us. We thank you for the knowledge that history goes through cycles as does much of the seasons, climate, and the universe. We thank you for our daily food and ask for its blessing. *Emenv.*

GREAT SPIRIT, ALMIGHTY HEALER, and Creator of all things, it is with a humbled heart that we gather together to offer up many thanks. We thank you for the buds that begin to appear upon the branches of the trees during the spring months. We thank you for the morning mist as it caresses the ground of the valleys near the running waters. We thank you for the dew that drips from the plants and herbs to give us the nourishment and cures we need for our bodies. We thank you for the germination and growth stages of the seed that reminds us of the life cycle of all living things. We thank you for the gift of life that the spring season reminds us of. We thank you for the unfolding of the petals of the daffodil and lily. We thank you for the moon that watches over us each night during our slumber. We thank you for your protection during our travels.

We ask for a greater awakening of spirits during these trying days. We ask for closed eyes to see, hardened hearts to loosen the chains of misinformation and mistrust as we begin the long, arduous task of bringing back balance. We ask for an end to bigotry, hatred, greed, and lust of both power and money. We ask for your healing hands to be placed upon those that are suffering from diverse diseases and disorders. We ask for guidance as we continue along our path. We ask for guidance, strength, and courage for those that continue to stand against injustice and the destruction of your creation. We ask for the salvation of those that are lost and deceived by the world. We ask for an end to homelessness and hunger. We ask for a stronger rising of spirit as we begin to replant, defend the defenseless, and bring back honor and courage to your people. We ask for an end to the stereotypes and hatred used to cause division among those that need to unite. We ask for freedom and an end to modern-day slavery that can be found throughout the four corners. We ask for the opening of doors where present ones begin to close. We ask for greater compassion be given to those that are aware of the poor and needy. We ask for a bountiful harvest for those that till the soil so they can feed the multitudes. We ask for greater understanding of the messages and signs that may be sent to us. We ask for rains to come to areas that are in great need. We ask for comfort for those that have lost loved ones. For those that have started their walk toward the spirit world, we ask for your guidance, strength, and courage. We ask for an end to the censorship displayed upon the social media sites and that this government provide a new Internet Bill of Rights to bring about much needed freedom of speech.

We thank you for our elders and the wisdom they provide us during our journey. We thank you for our children that will continue to build upon the foundation this generation has erected. We thank you for our earth that gives us the waters to hydrate us, foods to nourish us, and cures for our ailments. We thank you for the knowledge that you use the most unlikely characters to bring about anointed leadership that will move your will forward. We thank you for sky that continues to protect us. We thank you for the nature that surrounds us and gives us peace in a troubled world. We thank you for the wisdom found deep within our hearts. We thank you for bringing this country back from disaster toward one of prominence and prosperity. May we, as a nation, turn from our ways and return our focus upon you and your teachings. *Emenv.*

Great Spirit, Almighty Healer, and Creator of all things seen and unseen, it is with humbled hearts that we unite together as one to offer up many thanks. From the babbling brooks to the cascading streams that bring tranquility to our soul, we thank you. We thank you for the season of reaping that shows not only the beauty of the changing leaf colors of the trees but also the knowledge that there is also beauty in death. For it is in the death of our shells that we transcend into a more beautiful place to continue on. We thank you for the clouds that bring not only the moisture for the soil but also the shade needed for the hot summer days. We thank you for the beauty above as we watch the soaring of the hawk and eagle. We thank you for the calls of the wolf and coyote during the midnight hour.

We ask for continued healing for those that suffer through the diverse diseases and disorders. May they find the cures awaiting them in nature. We ask during this time of violence that guidance, courage, and strength be given to the leaders of the many lands to combat evil within their own countries. We ask for an end to those groups that wantonly destroy not only the land around them, but to your children as well. We ask for decisive action be placed against those that choose to force their will around the world, leaving free will by the wayside. We ask for a time where love transcends all and peace reigns throughout the four corners. We ask for an era where understanding and forgiveness is commonplace. We ask for a bountiful harvest season to bring food to those that are in great need. We ask for blessings to be poured out to those that stand against those that willfully destroy your creation through mining, fracking, drilling, and clear-cutting of our trees. We ask for your guidance each day so we may perform the works that we were assigned from the beginning. We ask for the release of all slaves that are still being used in the world. We ask for an end to the addictions that keep us from doing the work we need to do. We ask for protection for all life that remain defenseless. We ask for protection for all your children during these turbulent times.

We thank you for our elders that continue to give us the wisdom of the ancestors and the lessons of life today. We thank you for our children that will take these and pass them onto the next generation. We thank you for the remembrance of the innocence we once had and the lessons we have learned through our many trials. We thank you for the precious gift given for all life that you have created. We thank you for your love, guidance, strength, forgiveness, and comfort given during our lifetimes. We remain thankful for all you have given and that which is yet to come. *Emenv.*

GREAT SPIRIT, ALMIGHTY HEALER, and Creator of all things, it is with humbled hearts that we gather together to offer up many thanks. We thank you for the sacredness of the soil we walk upon, as it holds the blood and history of our ancestors. We thank you for the wisdom that comes to our hearts through the experiences we encounter as well as when we receive them from the Sacred Spirit within. We thank you for the strength found in the wind as it swirls in circles and the gentleness of the breeze as it gently caresses our cheeks. We thank you for the seasons that show us how life also moves through cycles. We thank you for the wisdom found in the trees when we learn to empty our minds and listen intently to the words they speak. We thank you for the lessons of the ant showing us the importance of working together.

We ask for healing for those that are enduring great suffering through diverse diseases and disorders. We ask for comfort and peace for those that have lost loved ones. We ask for strength and courage for those that have moved on to the spirit world. We ask for courage and a greater spiritual revival so we may become a greater voice that will not falter throughout the four corners. We ask for an end to the hatred that further destroys us. We ask instead for an era of peace where all become truly equal. We ask for an end to greed and materialistic desires. May we begin to think about others more than ourselves. We ask for closed eyes to see and hardened hearts to soften so we may begin to understand the destruction we have made and the task that lies before us. We ask for courage, strength, and guidance to espouse your words to those that you bring along our path. We ask for strong and clear eyes to keep watch for the signs of your return. We pray for our enemies so they may come to know you as your believers do. We ask for strength, guidance, and direction to endure and overcome our weaknesses. We again ask for rain to come to those areas being destroyed by fire or drought. We ask for patience when we tend to be impatient during our daily life. We ask for mercy and pray that your children will be found worthy to join you in the clouds.

We thank you for our elders and the wisdom they provide. May they be respected as they should. We thank you for our children that will build upon an unbreakable foundation this generation lays before them. We thank you for the many trials we endure to strengthen our spirit. We thank you for our relations that provide insight when it is needed. We thank you for the rains that come to bring growth and purification to the areas of need. We thank you for the precious gift of life and the magnificence of the beauty that surrounds us. We thank you for your listening and answering of our prayers. *Emenv.*

GREAT SPIRIT, ALMIGHTY HEALER, and Creator of all things, it is with humbled hearts that we unite together to offer up many thanks. We thank you for the meticulousness of your creation within the human body and the bodies of all living things. We thank you for wisdom and knowledge we come across when we spend time in nature. We thank you for the rushing waters that cascade down from the mountaintops that hydrate the bodies of all living things. We thank you for our daily food and ask for its blessing. We thank you for the rain forests as they supply us with the air to breathe. We thank you for the beauty that surrounds us, from each blade of grass to the peaks of every mountain.

We ask for continued healing for those that are suffering from diverse diseases and disorders. We are a weary people, Father, of the hatred, greed, lust of power that permeates from the wealthy and the governments of all nations. We are tired of those in our governments that do not represent the hearts and minds of their people. We ask for a greater unity among your people so we may begin the arduous task of repairing what we have nearly destroyed. You have tried to guide this generation to building a firm foundation for the next to build upon, and we ask for your strength and further guidance to accomplish this. We ask for protection, courage, and strength for those that are now taking a stand to protect the waters, land, and air. We ask for strength when we become surrounded by those that know only negativity in life. We ask for a time of repose where we can clear our minds and bring back the fire within our spirit. We ask for comfort and guidance also for those that have lost their way. We ask for signs and words to be given to those that do not believe your existence. We ask for blessings for those that have great faith in you. We ask for healing for those that have endured violence and abuse in their lives. We ask for protection and strength for those that continue to endure these horrendous acts.

We thank you for our elders and the lessons they have given. May we continue to honor them with the deepest respect. We thank you for our children that will one day take over and lead your people. We thank you for your many blessings and gifts that you have bestowed upon your children. We thank you for all answered prayers. We thank you for the precious gift of life and the reminder that all life is sacred. We thank you for our animal friends in nature that show us the true meaning of life and the wisdom that comes when we learn to watch and listen. *Emenv.*

GREAT SPIRIT, ALMIGHTY HEALER, and Creator of all things, we gather together this day with humbled hearts to offer up many thanks. We thank you for all two-leggeds, four-leggeds, swimmers, fliers, and crawlers. We thank you for the wisdom found in nature and through the many experiences we have faced along our journey. We thank you for the howls of the coyotes of the desert and the wolves of the forests. We thank you for the bees that pollinate the plants and the ants that aerate the soil. We thank you for the gift of life and the many blessings you have bestowed upon your children. We thank you for our thorns as they prevent us from becoming too boastful and proud.

We ask for a brief pause during this time of great spiritual awakening to bring forth purification. We ask for an end to the division among the people and the opening of closed eyes so they may see the deception placed upon them by their governments. We ask for all veils of secrecy to be lifted where nothing is ever again allowed to happen without the knowledge of the people. We ask for an end to the greed that permeates throughout the four corners and the lust of materialistic desires be laid waste. We ask for true equality where no one person is more powerful than the next. We ask for an end to all hostilities and wars in a world where the people are weary. We ask instead for an era of peace among all nations. We ask for your healing hands to be placed upon those that are suffering through physical and mental diseases and disorders. We ask for your hands to guide surgeons as they operate on those in operating rooms this day. We ask for young men who have sired and turned away from their children to understand the gift they were given and the responsibility they have to raise them. We ask for an end to modern-day slavery and the release of those that have been subjected to abuse and violence. We ask for protection for our children that have been abducted and lost in human trafficking. May they be found and brought back home to their loved ones.

We thank you for our elders and the lessons they teach us today as well as the wisdom of the ancestors. We thank you for our children that remind us of the innocence and the lessons we have long forgotten. May we continue to strengthen the foundation set forth by the seventh generation so they may have an unbreakable foundation to build upon. We thank you for our fathers and mothers that raise their children with righteousness and have prepared them for their adult life ahead. We thank you for our daily food and ask for its blessing. We thank you for the waters that hydrate us. We thank you for your love and your forgiveness when we stray from our path. *Emenv.*

GREAT SPIRIT, ALMIGHTY HEALER, and Creator of all things, it is with humbled hearts that we gather together to offer up many thanks. We thank you for the wisdom that comes to our hearts through the experiences we encounter as well as when we receive them from the spirit within. We thank you for the strength found in the wind as it swirls in circles and the gentleness of the breeze as it gently caresses our cheeks. We thank you for the swimmers that maneuver about in the lakes and streams. We thank you for the knowledge and wisdom found when we step away from our concrete jungles and observe nature in their own habitat.

We ask for healing for those that are enduring great suffering through diverse diseases and disorders. We ask for comfort and peace for those that have lost loved ones. We ask for strength and courage for those that have moved on to the spirit world. We ask for a greater spiritual revival so we may become a greater voice that will not falter throughout the four corners. We ask for an end to the hatred that continues to damage our souls. We ask instead for an era of peace where all become truly equal. We ask for an end to greed and materialistic desires. We ask for closed eyes to see and hardened hearts to soften so we may begin to understand the destruction we have made and the task that lies before us. We ask for protection for the defenseless. We ask for strong and clear eyes to keep watch for the signs of your return. We pray for our enemies so they may come to know you as your followers do. We ask for greater understanding of your words.

We thank you for our elders and the wisdom they provide. May they be respected as they should. We thank you for our children that take the time to observe the nature around them. We thank you for the many trials we endure that strengthen our spirit. We thank you for our relations that provide insight when it is needed. We thank you for the rains that come to bring growth and purification to the areas of need. We thank you for the precious gift of life and the magnificence of the beauty that surrounds us. We thank you for our thorns that keep us from becoming boastful and proud. *Emenv.*

Great Spirit, Almighty Healer, and Creator of all things, it is with a humbled heart that we gather together to offer up many thanks. We thank you for the morning mist as it caresses the soil of the valleys near the running waters. We thank you for the gift of life that the spring season reminds us of. We thank you for the light of the moon that watches over us each night during our slumber. We thank you for your protection during our travels. We thank you for the life cycle of all living things. For the gracefulness of the waves that flow across the sand to the crashing upon the rocky shore, we thank you. We thank you for the fruit of the tree and the vine. We thank you for the swaying of the palm leaves as the warm tropical winds flow through the land. We thank you for the knowledge that there is much more to your creation than what our eyes behold.

We continue to ask for a greater spiritual revival during these days. We ask for closed eyes to see, hardened hearts to loosen the chains of misinformation and mistrust as we begin the long, arduous task of bringing back balance. We ask for an end to bigotry, hatred, greed, and lust of both power and money. We ask for your healing hands to be placed upon those that are suffering from diverse diseases and disorders. We ask for guidance as we continue along our path. We ask for guidance, strength, and courage for those that continue to stand against injustice and the destruction of your creation. We ask for an era of peace where all people are truly equal and generosity abounds. We ask for an end to homelessness and hunger. We ask for a stronger rising of spirit as we begin to replant, defend the defenseless, and bring back honor and courage to your people. We ask for an end to the stereotypes and hatred used to cause division among those that need to unite. We ask for freedom for those that have been incarcerated for crimes that they did not commit. We ask for freedom for those abused and an end to modern-day slavery that can be found throughout the four corners. We ask for the opening of doors where present ones begin to close. We ask for greater compassion be given to those that are aware of those in need. We ask for a bountiful harvest for those that till the soil so they can feed the multitudes. We ask for rains to come to areas of drought. We ask for guidance each day as we continue along our path. We ask for greater understanding of the messages and signs that may be sent to us. We ask for a thorough cleansing of our feet so we may go where we are meant to go; our hands so we may create beauty; our hearts so we may better understand its messages; our eyes so we may behold the glory of your creation.

We thank you for our children that are willing to listen to the lessons, stories, and wisdom provided by our elders. We thank you for the earth that gives us the waters to hydrate us, foods to nourish us, and cures for our ailments. We thank you for the sky above that continues to protect us from the hazards of the second heaven. We thank you for the nature that surrounds us and gives us peace in a troubled world. *Emenv.*

GREAT SPIRIT, ALMIGHTY HEALER, and Creator of all things, it is with a humbled heart that we gather together to offer up many thanks. We thank you for the warmth of the sun during the day and the coolness of the moon during the night. We thank you for the many herbs and plants that provide us with cures for our ailments and diseases and for the nourishment that is given. We thank you for the waters that flow from the mountaintops that hydrate our bodies. We thank you for the trees and the rain forests that give us the air to breathe. We thank you for the gentle wind that soothes our spirits and the music it brings. We thank you for the peace that can be found in the nature that surrounds us. We thank you for the sacred circle that can be found throughout your creation, from the vastness of the universe around us to the very core of our earth. We thank you for the wisdom and our moral code kept within our hearts. We thank you for the cycles of climate and the four seasons. For the rains that come to areas of arid land, we thank you.

We ask for healing for those that are suffering through diverse diseases and disorders. We ask for your hands to be placed upon the surgeons that will be operating in emergency rooms this day. We ask for comfort and guidance for those that are low in spirit. We ask for a great revival of spiritual awakening during this time of turmoil and distress. We ask for protection for our animal friends, the bear, the wolf, the horse, the buffalo, the whale, and the dolphin that are facing grave danger from those that do not understand how precious all life is. We ask for protection, guidance, and strength as we stand against those that willfully destroy more of your creation. We ask for an end to the greed, corruption, lust of power and wealth that is found in our governments. We ask for protection of all sacred lands.

We ask for an era of peace in a world that is weary of war and those that sanction them. We ask for the veils of secrecy to continue to be lifted so the people will begin to understand and make informed decisions. We ask for closed eyes to open, hardened hearts to soften, and clogged ears to loosen in a time where unity of the four colors is needed. We ask for an end to the division that separates us and slows down the unity we need to bring back balance to an unbalanced world. We ask for greater compassion for those less fortunate than ourselves. We ask for a rich bounty of food that will allow all people to be fed.

We thank you for our elders that bring us wisdom, life lessons, culture and heritage awareness, and the stories from long ago. We thank you for our children that will take the lessons and wisdom they learn from us onto the next generation. We thank you for the great expanse of the universe that surround us and is the very center of our being. We thank you for our ancestors that remain with us from the spirit world to help us during our journey. We thank you for your forgiveness when we stray. We thank you for your love and guidance given to us each day. We thank you for the many gifts and blessings you have bestowed upon us. We thank you for the knowledge that life is embodied in everything you have created. We thank you for all answered prayers. We thank you for your love, forgiveness, mercy, and blessings. *Emenv.*

GREAT SPIRIT, ALMIGHTY HEALER, and Creator of all things, it is with humbled hearts that we unite together to offer up many thanks. We thank you for the spirit that dwells within our hearts and the hearts of all living things. We thank you for our ancestors that are still with us in spirit and the wisdom they have brought to us. We thank you for all two-leggeds, four-leggeds, swimmers, fliers, and crawlers that are with us. We thank you for the music found in the gentle winds that flow through the trees and the flowing waters. We thank you for the trials we endure to strengthen us and prepare us for what lies ahead. We thank you for the many answered prayers. We thank you for the gracefulness of the ocean waves as they gently caress the sandy shore. For the swaying of the palm and willow during the afternoon wind, we thank you. We thank you for the golden colors of the morning sunrise to the reddish hues of the evening setting. We thank you for the redwoods that stretch out toward the second heaven, displaying beauty under its canopy.

We ask for your healing hands to be placed upon those that are suffering from man-made and natural diseases and disorders. We ask for patience when we become agitated while we await the answering of our prayers. We ask for an end to the turmoil that has kept your people divided for too long. We ask for an end to such hatred, greed, lust of power and materialism that is found in our governments and corporations that have filled the hearts of those that have become complacent and naive. We ask for freedom for those that have been abducted or taken from their homes without cause. We ask for protection for your forests, waters, plains, and deserts that man has taken parts of your creation without replacing. We ask for strength, guidance, and courage for those that stand against governments that do not protect the lands or the treaties they have signed. We ask for protection for all two-leggeds, four-leggeds, swimmers, fliers, and crawlers that are facing grave danger. May we be of strong heart and defend all that are defenseless. We ask for guidance each day so we may travel our paths with courage, strong legs, and straight eyes. We ask for more compassion to be placed upon the hearts of those that are aware of the homeless in their cities.

We thank you for our elders that show us many life lessons and wisdom to carry within us during our journey. May we always endeavor to bring great honor to them. We thank you for our children that continue to teach us innocence and lessons long forgotten. May we provide them with an unbreakable foundation from which they will build on. We thank you for those in the military that keep us safe and for the sacrifice they and their families endure. We thank you for our relations that interact with us during the day that strengthen our spirits. We thank you for the gift of life and the paths you have given us. We thank you for the wisdom of the heart. May we learn to listen intently before we speak and understand that there is strength in silence. *Emenv.*

GREAT SPIRIT, ALMIGHTY HEALER, and Creator of all things, it is with a humbled heart that we gather together to offer up many thanks. We thank you for the many gifts and blessings that you have bestowed upon your children. May we use them for the betterment of all. We thank you for our trials that help to strengthen our spirits. We thank you for your forgiveness when we have strayed from our path and have caused disappointment. We thank you for our elders and the life lessons they have given us to assist us on our journey. We thank you for our children that will take these lessons and build upon the unbreakable foundation this generation will leave them.

We ask for continued healing for those afflicted with diverse diseases and disorders. For those undergoing surgery, we ask for your guiding hands to be placed on the surgeons during their operations. We ask for protection for those that are suffering through domestic violence and abuse. For those that have lost loved ones, we ask for comfort to be granted. We ask for guidance, strength, and courage for those that have crossed over into the spirit world and their next phase of life. We ask for an ease of tensions and divisions that separate us from our brothers. We ask for protection for our animal brothers—the wolf, bear, horse, buffalo, whale, and dolphin. We ask for greater understanding that all life is precious and sacred. We ask for an end to environmental abuse and destruction. May we strive to replace all that has been taken from our earth. We ask for greater awareness and compassion toward the homeless and the poor. We ask for open doors to those that are seeking work. We ask for an end to the materialistic desires that control us. We ask for a time of true equality where no one is more powerful than the next. We ask for an era of peace and tranquility where all four colors are able to unite for the common good. We ask for a greater spiritual awakening during this time of purification so we may begin the arduous task for restoring balance to ourselves, the earth, and strengthening the spirit that dwells in all your children.

We thank you for the early morning mists as it floats down from above. We thank you for the morning breeze that caresses our cheeks and brings a sense of peace to our spirit. We thank you for the wisdom that can be found in nature that will find its way into our hearts. We thank you for our ancestors that continue to watch over us from the spirit world. We thank you for the rainforests that provide us with the air to breathe. We thank you for the beauty of the autumn leaves to the budding of the leaves in the spring. We thank you for all answered prayers. We thank you for the guidance you provide as we begin a new day. *Emenv.*

GREAT SPIRIT, ALMIGHTY HEALER, and Creator of all things, we unite together with humbled hearts to offer up many thanks. We thank you for the rising of the sun as it lights up our path and provides warmth. We thank you for the moon as it watches over us during our slumber. We thank you for the sky that protects us each day and night. We thank you for the earth that supplies us with all that we need to survive. We thank you for the gift of life that you have breathed in to every living thing. We thank you for the sounds of the frogs, crickets, and grasshoppers; music of the wren and finch. We thank you for the soaring of the hawk and the eagle overhead. We thank you for the swaying of the grasslands of the plains as the afternoon breeze flows through the land. We thank you for the majestic mountains as they tower over the valleys. We thank you for the soft sands upon the shore and the gracefulness of the waves of the ocean waters.

We have allowed materialistic greed and money to control us. We ask for your forgiveness and guidance toward returning to a time when we were better caretakers of your creation. We have polluted the lands, waters, and skies and have brought hatred, corruption, and division where we were once united in tolerance. We ask for a return to an era of peace where all people are truly equal and we use the gifts provided to bring back balance to a world that is destroying itself. We have at times focused upon the wills of the flesh rather than keeping our focus upon you. We ask for your forgiveness and guidance. We ask for protection for our animal brothers and sisters facing grave danger from men that lost all understanding and love of life. We ask for protection for the women and children that continue to suffer through violence and abuse. We ask for strength, guidance, and courage as we stand against those that would continue to destroy the lands, waters, and skies above. We ask for an end to the corruption, greed, lust of power and wealth of those that are supposed to serve their people. We ask for an end to the division that continues to keep your people from uniting and fulfilling the prophecies. We ask for the release of all your children that have been incarcerated for crimes they did not commit. We ask for a time for boys to become men and become real fathers to the children they have sired. We ask for hardened hearts to soften and compassion be used to help the poor, homeless, widows, and all that are in need. We ask for your guidance each day.

We thank you for our many trials as they bring strength to our spirits. We thank you for our elders as they bring us the instruction and wisdom needed to follow our path. We thank you for our children that will build upon the foundation we have set before them. We thank you for our relations that interact with us each day to give us insight in areas of misunderstanding. We thank you for our family and friends that give us the support we need along our journey. We thank you for the knowledge that every living thing is unique and each has a specific purpose. We thank you for the many blessings and gifts you have given us. *Emenv.*

About the Author

DENNIS BINNS RETIRED AFTER twenty years in the military as a data systems technician, troubleshooting and repair of electronic systems. His travels took him to several countries in both the Pacific and Indian Oceans. During that time, he was getting to know diverse cultures and people while making friendships along the way. It is important for him to gain understanding of their hopes and desires that may contrast with his own.

Outside of the military, he has acted in community theaters, sang as a lead singer for a chapter of the group Up with People, and performed in a jazz band. He has worked in city government as an office clerk, managed a truck stop convenience store, hired as a maintenance man in a Baptist Church.

He married his wife, Mai, of thirty-three years before her passing. He has six children, thirteen grandchildren, and seven great-grandchildren.

He remains active in online social media. It is on Facebook that his followers encouraged him to write. This is an area that he was not accustomed to but decided to pursue for them. Deeply spiritual in nature, he found it was easier to have the Spirit write for him instead. He is a man of few words but the Spirit has many.

Compassion is an extremely important factor in his daily life. Giving to those less fortunate than himself is what drives him each day. Whether it is volunteering in the community or donating to certain charities, he is there giving as much as he is able. He is currently the chaplain for the Whitetop Tribe in Clay County, Kentucky.

CPSIA information can be obtained
at www.ICGtesting.com
Printed in the USA
LVHW070212140819
627592LV00016B/297/P